Forgiveness and mercy

Forgiveness and mercy

JEFFRIE G. MURPHY

ARIZONA STATE UNIVERSITY

and

JEAN HAMPTON

CAMBRIDGE
UNIVERSITY PRESS

PUBLISHED BY THE PRESS SYNDICATE OF THE UNIVERSITY OF CAMBRIDGE
The Pitt Building, Trumpington Street, Cambridge CB2 1RP, United Kingdom

CAMBRIDGE UNIVERSITY PRESS
The Edinburgh Building, Cambridge CB2 2RU, UK   http://www.cup.cam.ac.uk
40 West 20th Street, New York, NY 10011-4211, USA   http://www.cup.org
10 Stamford Road, Oakleigh, Melbourne 3166, Australia

First published 1988
First paperback edition 1990
Reprinted 1994, 1998

Typeset in Palatino

A catalogue record for this book is available from the British Library

Library of Congress Cataloguing-in-Publication Data is available

ISBN 0-521-39567-4 paperback
Transferred to digital printing 2002

Dedicated to
Lewis White Beck
and to
William and Elizabeth Hampton

Contents

Preface and acknowledgments

This book grew out of conversations and correspondence that we have had since 1985. At that time Murphy sent Hampton a copy of his 1982 essay "Forgiveness and Resentment" (a version of which is included as Chapter 1 of the present book). This prompted her to read, reflect on and write about the issues he had raised. After some initial correspondence and conversations that mixed philosophical topics and life experiences, we realized that we had a deep interest, both intellectual and personal, in the emotions of resentment, hatred and compassion and in the virtues of forgiveness and mercy – virtues that are often regarded as exemplifying the latter emotion and allowing us to overcome the former two. We found these topics important, not only for ethical theory and the theory of virtue, but also for social, political and legal philosophy. Moreover we also found that we both had personal reasons for wanting to subject to philosophical reflection emotions that were important parts of our own personalities and that engaged the religious and moral traditions in which we had been raised.

We early realized that we approached these topics in a sufficiently similar manner that useful exchange between us was possible; but we also realized that each would never bring the other around to a common point of view. We thought this tension between our views – within the bounds of general sympathy – might be illuminating to others, and thus the idea of the present book was born. We have no illusions that we have written a comprehensive and final treatise on the topics in question, but we do hope that between us we have placed enough interesting and important ideas on the table to have at least started a fruitful philosophical discussion.

The book is not, in any strict sense, a dialogue. What each author has done is to use the other's preceding chapter as a springboard from which to explore further dimensions of the topics under discussion. We used, as our model for such an approach, the book *Sense and Delusion* by Ilham Dilman and D. Z. Phillips (London: Routledge & Kegan Paul, 1971). In this stimulating book on the meaning of life, the authors react to each other, not with attempts at line-by-line commentary or refutation, but in ways that build on previous discussions to enrich and deepen the exploration of the important issues. This too has been our goal, and only the reader can determine the degree to which it has been attained.

One might also say that the history and form of the book are a kind of experiment on our part about how to do philosophy. We have engaged in a less lonely and more collaborative style of research in this volume than is usual in philosophy today. We commend it to others as potentially more fruitful, in at least some cases, than the independent but isolated toil we are generally expected to undertake.

The first person I must thank is Jeffrie Murphy himself, who came up with the idea that we might write a book with this format, and whose essay "Forgiveness and Resentment" was the catalyst for my thinking on these matters.

Portions of Chapters 2 and 4 were read at the University of Pittsburgh, the 1987 Pacific Meeting of the Society of Christian Philosophers, George Washington University's conference on "Causes of Quarrel" in June of 1987, and the California Institute of Technology in November of 1987. I am grateful to members of these audiences for comment and criticism, particularly to Richard Gale.

I wish to thank members of my graduate seminar at UCLA in the winter of 1987, especially Julie Heath-Elliot and Roger Florka, and members of my freshman seminar at Pittsburgh in the fall of 1987 for their reactions to many of the ideas in this book. I also thank Paul Deary for preparing the book's index and for help in proofreading.

My husband, Richard Healey, patiently waded through an alarming number of drafts of these chapters, with suggestions for improvement that were generally heeded and deeply appreciated.

Finally, I thank my parents, William and Elizabeth Hampton. In Deuteronomy parents are commanded to teach their children to love the Lord their God with all their hearts and minds and souls. This my parents did in the midst of a kind and loving environment, so that when I grew up and things became much harder, I had a rock to sustain me. Hence I dedicate my portion of the book to them.

JEAN HAMPTON
Pittsburgh, Pennsylvania

Portions of Chapter 1 originally appeared as "Forgiveness and Resentment" in *Minnesota Studies in Philosophy*, Volume VII, *Social and Political Philosophy*, edited by Peter A. French, Theodore E. Uehling, Jr., and Howard K. Wettstein (Minneapolis: University of Minnesota Press, 1982), and portions of Chapter 5 originally appeared as "Mercy and Legal Justice" in *Social Philosophy and Policy*, 4 (Autumn 1986). I am grateful to the University of Minnesota Press for permission to reprint the former and to Basil Blackwell for permission to reprint the latter.

A version of Chapter 3 was read at the 1988 Pacific Meeting of the Society of Christian Philosophers and at the 1988 Bowling Green Conference on "Liability in Law and Morals." I am grateful for discussion I was accorded at both meetings and particularly to James G. Hanink, who was my commentator at the former.

Several persons were generous enough to comment on all or part of my chapters, and I would like to take this opportunity to thank them for the help that their comments provided: Lewis Beck, Linell Cady, Bettie Anne Doebler, Antony Duff, Kent Greenawalt, Gareth Matthews, Jerome Neu, Robert Solomon, Peter Westen and – of course – Jean Hampton. Patricia Rohrbacker provided cheerful help in correcting the proof, and she also raised insightful questions about material in earlier drafts. I am grateful for her assistance. As usual, my wife, Ellen Canacakos, provided valuable conversations and insights on the topics of my philosophical reflections; I thank her for this and for so many other things.

Finally, I would like to convey special thanks to Lewis White Beck. He has been a constant source of inspiration and encouragement in my work since the days I studied Kant with him at the University of Rochester. His kind words in support of my earliest writings on the topic of forgiveness were instrumental in my deciding to keep on writing about this and related topics, and his comments on what I have written – including his comments on earlier drafts of much in the present volume – have been of great value to me. He has been my teacher, my mentor, and my friend; and I dedicate my portion of this book to him.

JEFFRIE G. MURPHY
Tempe, Arizona

Introduction

I. THE RETRIBUTIVE EMOTIONS

Jeffrie Murphy

Whoever has done me harm must suffer harm; whoever has put out my eye must lose an eye; and whoever has killed must die. This is an emotion, and a particularly violent one, and not a principle. . . . Retaliation does no more than ratify and confer the status of law on [this] pure impulse of nature.

Albert Camus, "Reflections on the Guillotine"

The critical legal studies movement has, in my judgment, raised at least one important issue for jurisprudence and moral philosophy. I am thinking of its claim that traditional moralistic jurisprudence errs in confining its inquiries to formal, abstract, and public doctrines and to the intellectual rationales for those doctrines. According to the "crits," a full philosophical grasp of law and morality requires an examination of the underlying causal forces that in part generate both the doctrines and the intellectual rationales for them. The person who seeks total enlightenment about morality and the law is invited to look, not just to the ideological superstructure, but to the underlying substructure that gives the superstructure at least a part of its point. This seems to me an invitation that those of us who practice traditional jurisprudence should accept.[1]

1 See Roberto Mangabeira Unger, *The Critical Legal Studies Movement* (Cambridge, Mass.: Harvard University Press, 1986). Unger attacks

1

Introduction

I am particularly interested in the degree to which certain moral and legal doctrines are rooted in specific *passions* (feelings, emotions) and the degree to which a philosophical examination of those passions will have a bearing on an understanding and evaluation of the doctrines that they in part generate and for which these doctrines in part serve as rationalizations. Although not currently at the center of philosophical fashion, this type of inquiry has, of course, a venerable philosophical history. It was pursued not simply by Nietzsche, Freud, Marx, and other heroes of the critical legal studies movement, but also by such writers as Hume and Adam Smith – pursued in their case as an inquiry into "the origin of our moral sentiments." Smith, for example, believed that much of our idea of retributive justice had to be understood in terms of the passion of resentment; and it is this family of passions, in fact, that I propose to take as my object of inquiry for the present study.[2]

Speaking very generally, we may say that the criminal law (among other things that it does) institutionalizes certain feelings of anger, resentment, and even hatred that we typically (and *perhaps* properly) direct toward wrongdoers, especially if we have been *victims* of those wrongdoers. (The great symbol for such institutionalization in our literature is that of Athena making an honorable home in Athens for the Furies and thereby transforming them into the Eumenides or "the kindly ones.") In the present age, most of us do not feel comfortable talking about the criminal law in such terms, for we are inclined to think that civilized people are not given to hatred and to an anger so intense that it generates the desire for revenge – that they are not, in short, driven by what (following Westermarck) I will call the "retributive emotions."[3]

what he calls the "formalism" and "objectivism" of traditional legal and moral theory.

2 See Adam Smith, *The Theory of Moral Sentiments* (1759; Indianapolis: Liberty Press, 1982), pp. 34–8 and 67–108.

3 See Edward Westermarck, *Ethical Relativity* (London: Routledge & Kegan Paul, 1932), Chapter 3. Westermarck's work on the moral emotions – particularly the retributive emotions – is interestingly discussed

2

Introduction

We prefer to talk high-mindedly of our reluctantly advocating punishment of criminals perhaps because social utility or justice demands it and tend to think that it is only primitives who would actually *hate* criminals and want them to suffer to appease an anger or outrage that is felt toward them. Good people are above such passions or at least they try to be. Some would even say that this is a requirement of Christianity.

It has not been this way in all ages, of course. Consider, for example, what James Fitzjames Stephen – the great Victorian judge and theorist of the criminal law – said about that branch of law and its relation to the retributive emotions. He was no doubt a devout Christian; but he could, to use the current vernacular, really "get into" hating. Though often regarding criminals as rather like noxious insects to be ground under the heel of society, Stephen did not see the punishment of such persons as having merely extermination value. The criminal law, he claimed, gives "distinct shape to the feeling of anger" and provides a "distinct satisfaction to the desire for vengeance." He wrote:

> The sentence of the law is to the moral sentiments of the public in relation to any offence what a seal is to hot wax. It converts into a permanent final judgment what might otherwise be a transient sentiment. . . . [T]he infliction of punishment by law gives definite expression and solemn ratification and justification to the hatred which is excited by the commission of the offence. . . . The forms in which deliberate anger and righteous disapprobation are expressed [in the execution of criminal justice] stand to the one set of passions in the same relation which marriage stands to [the sexual passions].[4]

Stephen's point is a simple one: Certain wrongdoers quite properly excite the resentment (anger, hatred) of all right-thinking people, and the criminal law is a civilized and effi-

in J. L. Mackie's "Morality and the Retributive Emotions," in his collection of essays *Persons and Values* (Oxford: Clarendon Press, 1985).
4 James Fitzjames Stephen, *A History of the Criminal Law of England* (London, 1883), Vol. II, pp. 81–2.

3

cient way in which such passions may be directed toward their proper objects, ⌐allowing victims to get legitimate revenge consistently with the maintenance of public order.⌐ This is not its only legitimate and important purpose, but it is one of them. Passions such as resentment can, of course, provoke irrational and dangerous conduct (which passions cannot?), but this is no more a reason for condemning them in principle than it would be for condemning the sexual passions. The case for the rational control and institutionalization of a passion must not, in short, be confused with a case for the utter condemnation and extinction of that passion.

The view expressed by Stephen, although it has a certain grim plausibility, bumps up against some other fairly widely held views in our culture – specifically the view that we should be moved, not merely by the hard passions of retribution, but also (or even primarily) by the softer feelings of compassion or love and that these feelings should at least temper the feelings that provoke a retributive response to wrongdoing. Such Christian virtues as forgiveness and mercy are thought to involve these soft feelings. Indeed such sentiments and virtues are sometimes taken to be characteristic of the Christian tradition and are often taken to show the moral advance that Christianity made over what ancient Greek culture had to offer – even at its best. The best of pagan culture – represented by Athena in the *Oresteia* - generally rises only to the procedural control of strict retributive justice but rarely even considers that such justice might be transcended by higher moral demands.[5] However, although the claims of compassion clearly have an important place in the Christian tradition, and with them the virtues of mercy and forgiveness, it would be a mistake to think that such concerns are unique to that tradition. Consider an example from the Jewish tradition: "Even God prays. What is His prayer? May it be My will that My love of compassion overwhelm my demand for strict justice."[6]

5 But see Aristotle's discussion of *epieikēs* (decent, equitable) at *Nicomachean Ethics*, Book V, Chapter 10.
6 Mahzor for Yom Kippur. The Rabbinical Assembly of New York, 439;

Thus several moral and religious traditions may come together on this issue and may, under the banner of counsels of forgiveness or mercy, suggest that the resentment that is in fact built into much of our moral and legal response to wrongdoing is inappropriate – either because we should never feel it at all or because we should always be readily open to the possibility of overcoming or transcending these feelings in the pursuit of the deeper values of love and compassion.

Given an assumption that Jean Hampton and I will make throughout the book – namely, that passions are at least in part cognitive states, states of *belief* and not just feeling – it is reasonable to suppose that some of the emotional tensions described above represent *intellectual* tensions, and thus reasonable to suppose that the gap between superstructure and substructure, between doctrine and underlying passion, is not as sharp as some seem to believe.[7] Thus there are issues

from Berakhot 7a. For a discussion of the view of forgiveness expounded in the classical Jewish sources, see Louis E. Newman's "The Quality of Mercy: On the Duty to Forgive in the Judaic Tradition," *Journal of Religious Ethics*, 15 (Fall 1987), pp. 155–72. The perspective on forgiveness in the present book is in some general sense Kantian (what some have called secularized Protestantism) – a perspective that places great emphasis on the value of individual autonomy and the voluntary (often quasi-contractual) nature of moral relations. According to Newman, the Jewish perspective on forgiveness has a different basis, for "within Judaism one is not an autonomous moral agent, but a member of a covenanted community" (p. 169).

7 Emotions, unlike such simple sensations as headaches, have a cognitive structure and are thus open, at least in part, to rational evaluation and control. Consider how emotions are differentiated – how we can explain the difference between such emotions as guilt, shame, resentment, jealousy, and fear. These are all simply ways of *feeling bad*, and thus the differences between them cannot be accounted for totally in terms of how each emotion subjectively feels. What, then, is the difference? Surely it is the belief, the cognitive state, that is the essential identifying part of each emotion – guilt as involving the belief that one has done something morally wrong; shame, the belief that one has fallen short of some ideal one has of oneself; resentment, the belief that one has suffered a moral injury; jealousy, the belief that one may lose a loved object to a rival; and fear, the belief that one is in danger. Some emotions are intrinsically irrational; e.g., phobias are irrational fears in

here that will profit from being *thought through* – questions that are philosophical (and not merely causal) in nature and that require philosophical analysis and theorizing. For example: When, if ever, is hatred or anger toward wrongdoers appropriate? When, if ever, should hatred be overcome by sympathy or compassion? What are forgiveness and mercy, and to what degree do they require – both conceptually and morally – the overcoming of certain passions (hatred perhaps) and the motivation by others (compassion perhaps)? If forgiveness and mercy are indeed moral virtues, what role – if any – should they play in the *law*?

In what follows, Jean Hampton and I take up these questions. I begin, in Chapter 1, with a discussion of forgiveness and resentment, and I argue that overcoming resentment in order to forgive can sometimes be morally inappropriate. In Chapter 2, Hampton develops a discussion of the differences between hatred and resentment, offering only lukewarm support for the latter and strongly opposing at least one variant of the former. In Chapter 3, I attempt a qualified defense of a kind of hatred that I believe her discussion leaves out and that I call "retributive hatred." Hampton follows in Chapter

---

the sense that they are directed to an object that is not in fact dangerous or reasonably believed to be so. (Nobody would call a person "phobic" who fears a hungry and aggressive tiger in the room with him.) The relation between rationality and emotions is in other cases more complex. Sometimes a person may be judged irrational, not because the emotion he experiences is itself irrational (like a phobia), but because of the *role* he allows certain emotions to play in his life. Spinoza, for example, does not regard as irrational a person who takes prudent precautions in attempting to avoid death (e.g., a person who looks both ways before crossing a street). He does, however, characterize as deeply irrational – as in "bondage" – a person who is "led" by the fear of death to such a degree that he misses out on the joys and benefits life has to offer. For more on this, see my "Rationality and the Fear of Death," *The Monist*, 59 (April 1976), reprinted in my collection of essays *Retribution, Justice, and Therapy: Essays in the Philosophy of Law* (Dordrecht: Reidel, 1979). Also see Robert Solomon, *The Passions* (Garden City, N.Y.: Anchor/Doubleday, 1976), and William Lyons, *Emotion* (Cambridge: Cambridge University Press, 1980), for a discussion of various theories of emotion (including Spinoza's) and for a defense of a cognitive theory.

4 by admitting the existence of a retributive idea that can sometimes be a legitimate response to wrongdoing, but she denies that this idea is a part of hatred. She then commends forgiveness in different circumstances than I do and introduces the topic of mercy. In the final chapter of the book I present a sustained discussion of mercy and compassion.

Before proceeding with this substantive inquiry, however, it might be worthwhile to pause for a moment and attempt to quell the doubts of a certain kind of skeptic about the legitimacy of the whole present endeavor. Who cares, this skeptic will charge, about the emotions anyway? Let us discard this concern along with other excessively Protestant concerns with "purity of heart" and confine our attentions to what really matters – namely, the *actions* that people perform and whether those actions are permissible or impermissible, just or unjust. This, our skeptic will argue, is the true business of morality – of that part of morality, at any rate, that has any bearing on law and society.

I take this skeptic seriously because he represents the voice of one of my own previous selves. When I first began to write on forgiveness and resentment it was in response to an invitation to contribute to a volume of essays on social and political philosophy. I had spent many years writing on the topic of criminal punishment and defending a generally retributive outlook on punishment.[8] Punishment is clearly an acceptable (traditional) topic in social and political philosophy, and one who thinks about the topic of punishment – the *hard* response to wrongdoing – will at some point naturally think about such *softer* responses as excuse, mercy, and forgiveness. As I started to think about forgiveness, however, I found that I was becoming more and more interested in it as a moral virtue, and I stopped caring directly about its social, political, and legal ramifications. I thus gave the editor of the volume the opportunity to withdraw his invitation – an offer that he kindly, if not wisely, refused. Thus I was left with the

---

8 See my *Retribution, Justice, and Therapy: Essays in the Philosophy of Law.*

feeling that the essay was going to appear in a collection where it simply did not belong, and I began to reflect on the grounds for my disquiet.

I have come to believe that this disquiet was unjustified. Many important social practices are direct outgrowths – in institutional form – of deep human passions or emotions. As noted earlier, punishment may in part be regarded as the institutionalization of such emotions as resentment and indignation. Insofar as our social and legal practices reflect our emotions, the examination of those emotions is not out of place as a part of the body of social and political philosophy.

But the relevance of the emotions is much deeper than this. It is a limitation of the liberal tradition to think that social and political matters are restricted to concerns with how we *act* – how we treat others and what we get to do. In this tradition, the concern with social and political philosophy is simply a concern with just rules of conduct. This concern is vitally important, of course, but it no more exhausts all of social and political value than it exhausts all of moral value; and thus, in focusing exclusively on this concern, the liberal tradition leaves out something of great social and political importance, something stressed by such otherwise diverse writers as Plato, Aristotle, Aquinas, Rousseau, Marx, Freud, and Marcuse. It is this: that one legitimate concern of politics and social life is a concern with what *kind of people* will grow up and flourish. Will their personalities be rich and full and integrated (*virtuous* in Aristotle's sense), or will they be stunted and limited and alienated?

The liberal tradition tends to ignore this issue because it tends to take passions or desires as givens, and sees politics and law as being concerned with the promotion of freedom where freedom is understood simply as the ability to obtain objects of desire without external impediment.[9] But there is

9 "Liberty, or freedom, signifieth, properly, the absence of opposition; by opposition, I mean external impediments of motion. . . . [T]he liberty of man . . . consisteth in this, that he finds no stop, in doing what he has the will, desire, or inclination to do." Thomas Hobbes, *Leviathan*, Part Two, Chapter 21.

a kind of slavery – slavery of the mind or personality – that no "Bill of Rights," no guarantees of external freedom, can correct. If we are in bondage to pointless or irrational or self-destructive passions, we lack what Spinoza thought of as *freedom of the mind*, perhaps the most important kind of freedom for a human being who would hope to be truly autonomous.

We are all, to a great extent, products of whatever system of socialization is operative in our culture. If this socialization process cultivates certain irrational or destructive or self-demeaning emotions within us, we will become prisoners to those emotions – no matter how free we may think ourselves in acting upon them without impediment. Similar harm will be done if our culture seeks to extinguish emotions that are in fact healthy and valuable – a worry later to be explored with respect to resentment and hatred. Thus it must be regarded as a relevant project within social and political and legal philosophy to examine the passions or emotions (such as resentment) in order at least to attempt to deal with the question of the degree to which, if at all, these passions or emotions should be reinforced, channeled in certain directions, or even eliminated where this is possible.[10]

Even liberal John Stuart Mill came to see the importance of this issue when he wrote his *Subjection of Women;* for he saw that women were enslaved as much by their feelings of subservience as by any external impediments to their actions. And when Marx claimed that religion is the opiate of the masses, he surely meant in part to suggest that Christianity has encouraged the development of meek and forgiving dispositions that will tolerate oppression, and that will call that toleration virtue. And when novelist Fay Weldon cries out against forgiveness, her point is in part a

10 I first came to see the importance of this kind of inquiry when I read Jerome Neu's insightful exploration of the personal, moral, and social dimensions of the emotions of jealousy and envy. See his "Jealous Thoughts," in *Explaining Emotions,* ed. Amelie Oksenberg Rorty (Berkeley: University of California Press, 1980). See also his *Emotion, Thought, and Therapy* (Berkeley: University of California Press, 1977).

feminist one: that women have been taught to forgive and accept when they should have been taught to resent and resist. Thus political and social and legal philosophy *must* concern itself with the passions – their nature, their justification, their proper scope and social influence, their possible control. The present set of reflections on forgiveness and resentment may be viewed as a part of social and political philosophy so conceived.

> Marat
> these cells of the inner self
> are worse than the deepest stone dungeon
> and as long as they are locked
> all your revolution remains
> only a prison mutiny
> to be put down
> by corrupted fellow prisoners
>   Peter Weiss, *Marat/Sade*

II. FORGIVENESS AND CHRISTIANITY

Jean Hampton

Jeffrie Murphy is a philosopher of law and I am a political philosopher. Hence, as his portion of this Introduction indicates, the discussions that follow are primarily informed by the theories and methodology of modern moral, political and legal philosophy. However, my interest in these topics also has a religious source, and this source provides another focus for the present book.

Like many who have been brought up in the Christian faith, I have frequently been told by clerics, Sunday school teachers and members of congregations that I must forgive those who have wronged me. One minister whom I recently heard give a sermon on the topic of forgiveness exhorted his congregation, which was to a fairly normal degree a resentful, indignant and hateful group of human beings, to engage in what he called an "orgy of forgiveness" and thereby do their part to realize God's peaceable kingdom on this earth. The congregation was dutiful in accepting the wisdom of the minister's message and for a while tried to be nicer to one another, but underneath this niceness they did not, to any significant degree, become any less resentful, indignant or hateful. Why, I wondered, do people accept with their heads, but not believe in their hearts, the Christian message of forgiveness?

The question took on new urgency after a particularly painful series of events beset my family and plunged us into what one might call an "orgy of resentment." What struck me about the anger we felt towards those who had wronged us was that it seemed entirely appropriate and certainly not anything we wanted to give up or overcome. I began to worry that Christianity nonetheless required me to forgive those who had wronged us, which, given their actions, I was loath to do.

It seemed that I had three ways of resolving my quandary. First, I could try to have it both ways and do what the congregation did, that is, agree that I should forgive them but still sustain my anger towards them by covering it up (a strategy which might deceive others, and even myself, that I had obeyed the commandment to forgive them). Second, I could reject – or at least try to reject – these emotions, and honestly follow the commandment. Or third, I could decide to reject the commandment and keep the emotions.

The first choice wasn't a serious option; apart from its dishonesty, it was in practice impossible since my anger was too intense to hide. But which of the other two should I choose? Was it even possible to follow the second, arguably Christian course, given the grip my anger had on me? My philosophical training finally came to the forefront. I should, I thought, follow – or at least try to follow – the commandment to forgive them if, *but only if*, the commandment was right. It was while I was in this frame of mind that Murphy sent me his essay on forgiveness, and it was that essay which launched the reflections in Chapter 2 and thus precipitated this book.

What is the conclusion of that inquiry? Is the Christian

commandment right? I found myself continually coming to its defense, and becoming increasingly critical of the kinds of anger that we victims generally feel towards those who wrong us. In my view, Camus's celebration of violent retaliation in the quotation at the beginning of this introduction is dead wrong – even dangerous. Against Murphy I will argue that this response should always be eschewed both by individuals and by legal systems. Nonetheless I also found myself refusing to endorse forgiveness as a virtue in *all* circumstances, and even commending a kind of hatred which I call 'moral hatred' as sometimes morally appropriate. Congregations who refuse to follow their ministers' injunctions to forgive wrongdoers can sometimes, I argue, be right.

Some Christians may find this conclusion offensive and unchristian, but while I acknowledge that it is not a traditional answer, I do attempt to argue that it is consistent with, and perhaps even encouraged by, the words and deeds of Jesus, who is frequently an angry man, reminding one of the Old Testament prophets. I make such arguments as a philosopher, and I come to grips with the Christian teachings and texts from outside the tradition of theological reflections on these subjects. But I hope that my perspective is of some interest to theologians and others, who may be intrigued by this treatment of biblical teachings as suggestive of reasoned arguments, and by the (sometimes iconoclastic) results of doing so.

Since I offer standard philosophical arguments for my positions on forgiveness, resentment, hatred and mercy, those readers who are not Christian can ignore, if they wish, any allusions to this tradition which those arguments contain. But since the Judeo-Christian tradition has played, and continues to play, an enormous role in influencing the political and legal institutions in which these emotions and virtues are given shape, it is at least fitting, and perhaps important, that the present discussion should include exploration of some parts of that tradition which bear on how we should respond to those who wrong us. Indeed, Jeffrie Murphy, whose perspective is largely secular, found himself discussing a number of New Testament passages in the chapter on forgiveness which begins this volume.

I also think Jesus' views on forgiveness, hatred and mercy are of interest to anyone who has been badly wronged by others (and which of us on this earth hasn't?). Not only are they unusual and provocative, but they are also intended to help those who are suffering. The reader may therefore find them of some use.

Chapter 1

Forgiveness and resentment

JEFFRIE MURPHY

Understand, and forgive, my mother said, and the
effort has quite exhausted me. I could do with some
anger to energize me, and bring me back to life again.
But where can I find that anger? Who is to help me?
My friends? I have been understanding and forgiving
my friends, my female friends, for as long as I can
remember. . . . Understand and forgive. . . .
Understand husbands, wives, fathers, mothers.
Understand dog-fights above and the charity box
below, understand fur-coated women and children
without shoes. Understand school – Jonah, Job and
the nature of the Deity; understand Hitler and the
bank of England and the behavior of Cinderella's sisters. Preach acceptance to wives and tolerance to husbands; patience to parents and compromise to the
young. Nothing in this world is perfect; to protest
takes the strength needed for survival. Grit your
teeth, endure. Understand, forgive, accept, in the
light of your own death, your own inevitable corruption. . . .
  Oh mother, what you taught me! And what a miserable, crawling, snivelling way to go, the worn-out
slippers neatly placed beneath the bed, careful not to
give offense.

Fay Weldon, *Female Friends*

To err is human; to forgive, supine.

S. J. Perelman

14

Forgiveness and resentment

Forgiveness, Bishop Butler teaches, is the forswearing of
resentment – the resolute overcoming of the anger and
hatred that are naturally directed toward a person who has
done one an unjustified and non-excused moral injury.[1] By
his emphasis on the forswearing of resentment, Butler indicates that he quite properly wants to draw a distinction
between forgiveness (which may be a virtue and morally
commanded) and forgetting (which may just happen).
Forgiveness is the sort of thing that one does for a reason,
and where there are reasons there is a distinction between
good ones and bad ones.

What, then, are the good reasons for forgiveness? Butler
has useful things to say in response to this question, but his
response is limited by a perspective that strikes me as too
consequentialist. Resentment, he argues, can provoke bad
consequences – especially such anti-social actions as personal
revenge. Forgiveness is thus justified primarily as a way of
avoiding such undesirable consequences. Resentment does
indeed perform a useful social job – the job of reinforcing the
rules of morality and provoking defenses of those rules – but
when it is allowed to range beyond this useful function, as
human weakness and vanity typically allow it to, it becomes
counterproductive and even seriously harmful to the social
fabric. Tendencies to forgive thus are to be supported to the
degree that they help individuals to overcome or avoid such
excesses.

This is surely part of the story, but – as Butler himself sometimes sees – there is considerably more to be told. Butler
stresses that the passion of resentment functions in a defensive role – defensive of the rules of morality and of the social
fabric those rules define. But he never fleshes out this insight
in sufficient detail adequately to highlight central features of

---

1 Joseph Butler, *Fifteen Sermons* (London, 1726), Sermon VIII, "Upon
   Resentment," and Sermon IX, "Upon Forgiveness of Injuries."

the context wherein resentment and forgiveness have their life.

In my view, resentment (in its range from righteous anger to righteous hatred) functions primarily in defense, not of *all* moral values and norms, but rather of certain *values of the self*. Resentment is a response not to general wrongs but to wrongs against oneself; and these resented wrongs can be of two sorts: resentment of direct violations of one's rights (as in assault) *or* resentment that another has taken unfair advantage of one's sacrifices by free riding on a mutually beneficial scheme of reciprocal cooperation. Only the immediate victim of crime is in a position to resent a criminal in the first way; all the law-abiding citizens, however, may be in a position to resent the criminal (and thus be secondary victims) in the second way – at least on Herbert Morris's well-known theory of such matters.[2]

I am, in short, suggesting that the primary value defended by the passion of resentment is *self-respect*, that proper self-respect is essentially tied to the passion of resentment, and that a person who does not resent moral injuries done to him (of either of the above sorts) is almost necessarily a person lacking in self-respect. Thus some of the primary reasons justifying forgiveness will be found, not in general social utility, but in reasons directly tied to an individual's self-respect or self-esteem, his perception of his own worth, of what he is owed. In some limited sense, then, I side with Stephen: Resentment (perhaps even some hatred) is a good thing, for it is essentially tied to a non-controversially good thing – self-respect. Let me elaborate on this a bit.

As noted by thinkers as otherwise diverse as Butler and Nietzsche, resentment has a very unattractive – even dangerous and unhealthy – dimension. This is something I would not want to deny. In addition to many of its other disadvantages, resentment can stand as a fatal obstacle to the restora-

2 Herbert Morris, "Persons and Punishment," *The Monist*, 52 (October 1968); reprinted in his collection of essays *Guilt and Innocence* (Berkeley: University of California Press, 1976).

tion of equal moral relations among persons, and thus it cannot always be the final "bottom line" as the response we take to those who have wronged us. Forgiveness heals and restores; and, without it, resentment would remain as an obstacle to many human relationships we value. This can be seen most clearly in such intimate relationships as love and friendship. The people with whom we are most intimate are those who can harm us the most, for they are the persons to whom we have let down our guard and exposed our vulnerabilities. Because of the nature of intimacy, moral injuries here tend to be not just ordinary injustices but also *betrayals*. Thus resentment here can be deep and nearly intractable – as revealed in the quip of Cosmus, Duke of Florence: "You shall read that we are commanded to forgive our enemies; but you never read that we are commanded to forgive our friends."[3] Deep as these hurts of intimacy may be, however, what would be the consequence of never forgiving any of them? Surely it would be this: the impossibility of ever having the kind of intimate relationships that are one of the crowning delights of human existence. The person who cannot forgive is the person who cannot have friends or lovers.

For this reason, it is easy to see why forgiveness is typically regarded as a virtue. Forgiveness is not always a virtue, however. Indeed, if I am correct in linking resentment to self-respect, a too ready tendency to forgive may properly be regarded as a *vice* because it may be a sign that one lacks respect for oneself. Not to have what Peter Strawson calls the "reactive attitude" of resentment when our rights are violated is to convey – emotionally – either that we do not think we have rights or that we do not take our rights very seriously.[4] Forgiveness may indeed restore relationships, but to seek restoration at all cost – even at the cost of one's very human dignity – can hardly be a virtue. And, in intimate relationships, it can hardly be true love or friendship either – the

---

3 Quoted in Francis Bacon's essay "Of Revenge" (1597).
4 Peter Strawson, "Freedom and Resentment," *Proceedings of the British Academy*, 1962.

kind of love and friendship that Aristotle claimed is an essential part of the virtuous life. When we are willing to be door-mats for others, we have, not love, but rather what the psychiatrist Karen Horney calls "morbid dependency."[5] If I count morally as much as anyone else (as surely I do), a failure to resent moral injuries done to me is a failure to care about the moral value incarnate in my own person (that I am, in Kantian language, an end in myself) and thus a failure to care about the very rules of morality.[6] To put the point in yet another way: If it is proper to feel *indignation* when I see third parties morally wronged, must it not be equally proper to feel *resentment* when I experience the moral wrong done to myself? Morality is not simply something to be believed in; it is something to be *cared* about. This caring includes concern about those persons (including oneself) who are the proper objects of moral attention.

Interestingly enough, a hasty readiness to forgive – or even a refusal to display resentment initially – may reveal a lack of respect, not just for oneself, but for others as well. The Nietzschean view, for example, is sometimes portrayed (perhaps unfairly) as this: There is no need for forgiveness, because a truly strong person will never feel resentment in the first place. Why? Because he is not so weak as to think that other people – even those who harm him – matter enough to have any impact on his self-respect. We do not resent the insect that stings us (we simply *deal* with it), and neither should we resent the human who wrongs us.[7]

5 Karen Horney, *Neurosis and Human Growth* (New York: Norton, 1950).
6 See Thomas E. Hill, Jr., "Servility and Self-Respect," *The Monist*, 57 (January 1973), pp. 87–104.
7 "To be incapable of taking one's enemies, one's accidents, even one's misdeeds seriously for very long – that is the sign of strong, full natures in whom there is an excess of the power to form, to mold, to recuperate and to forget. . . . Such a man shakes off with a single shrug many vermin that eat deep into others." Friedrich Nietzsche, *On the Genealogy of Morals*, Essay I, Section 10 (p. 39 of the Walter Kaufmann translation; New York: Random House, 1967).
    According to Paul Lauritzen, a similar indifference to injury by others (a refusal to view it as genuine injury) can be found in some strands of Christianity. If one believes that the Kingdom of God is imminent,

Although there is something attractive and worth discussing about this view, most of us would probably want to reject it as too demeaning of other human beings and our moral relations with them. I shall thus for the present assume the following: Forgiveness is acceptable only in cases where it is consistent with self-respect, respect for others as responsible moral agents, and allegiance to the rules of morality (i.e., forgiveness must not involve complicity or acquiescence in wrongdoing).[8]

II. THE NATURE AND JUSTIFICATION OF FORGIVENESS

Enough by way of introduction. Having presented an overview of the problem of forgiveness, let me now move to a more detailed consideration of the two basic questions concerning forgiveness: (1) What is forgiveness; that is, how is the concept to be analyzed and distinguished from other concepts with which it may be confused? and (2) when, if at all,

interests and well-being become radically redefined; and, since earthly injury is no longer counted as harm, there is no occasion for resentment. See Paul Lauritzen, "Forgiveness: Moral Prerogative or Religious Duty?" *Journal of Religious Ethics*, 15 (Fall 1987), pp. 141–54. Socrates also poses an interesting case here. On his stated view (in *Apology*, for example) a good person cannot be harmed or injured. Thus, if one regards oneself as a good person, then one – though positively brimming over with self-respect – will presumably never have occasion to resent, because one will never regard oneself as having been injured in any morally relevant way. Given the degree to which Socrates dealt with his enemies with ridicule and sarcasm, it is by no means clear that he actually practiced what he preached in this regard. Neither is it clear that the view he advocated is unambiguously desirable – even as an ideal. Could this level of insulation from others be compatible with true love or friendship or meaningful membership in any human relationship or community, for example? For an exploration of some of these issues, see my "Violence and the Socratic Theory of Legal Fidelity," in my collection *Retribution, Justice, and Therapy: Essays in the Philosophy of Law* (Dordrecht: Reidel, 1979), pp. 40–57.

8   For a discussion of the ways in which forgiveness may involve complicity in wrongdoing, see Aurel Kolnai's "Forgiveness," *Proceedings of the Aristotelian Society*, 1973–4; reprinted in his collection of essays *Ethics, Value, and Reality* (Indianapolis: Hackett, 1978).

is forgiveness justified? (If it is never justified, then a tendency to bestow it can surely not be a virtue.)

First the question of meaning. I have already indicated, following Butler, that ⌈forgiveness⌉ essentially involves an attempt to overcome resentment. This feature allows us to distinguish forgiveness from three other concepts with which it is often confused: *excuse*, *justification*, and *mercy*. To excuse is to say this: What was done was morally wrong; but, because of certain factors about the agent (e.g., insanity), it would be unfair to hold the wrongdoer responsible or blame him for the wrong action. To justify is to say this: What was done was *prima facie* wrong; but, because of other morally relevant factors, the action was – *all* morally relevant factors considered – the right thing to do. And why is neither of these forgiveness? Because we may forgive only what it is initially proper to resent; and, if a person has done nothing wrong or was not responsible for what he did, there is *nothing to resent* (though perhaps much to be sad about). Resentment – and thus forgiveness – is directed toward *responsible wrongdoing*; and therefore, if forgiveness and resentment are to have an arena, it must be where such wrongdoing remains intact - i.e., neither excused nor justified. ("Father forgive them for they know not what they do" would go better as "Father *excuse* them for they know not what they do.")

Forgiveness is also not mercy. To be merciful is to treat a person less harshly than, given certain rules, one has a right to treat that person. For example, the rules of chivalry give me the right to kill you under certain circumstances of combat. If you beg for mercy, you are begging that I do something less severe than kill you. When Portia advises Shylock to show mercy, she is asking that he accept a payment less harsh than the one that, given the terms of his bargain, he has a right to demand. Three things are present in such cases: some notion of just or rightful authority, some notion of the supplicant's having fallen afoul of certain public rules, and the consideration of a certain external action (a killing, a payment of a "pound of flesh"). None of these is necessarily involved in forgiveness. Forgiveness is primarily a matter of how I *feel* about you (not how I treat you), and thus I may forgive you in my heart of hearts or even after you are dead. (I cannot show you mercy in my heart of hearts or after you are dead, however.) I may think I have forgiven you; but, when old resentments rise up again, I may say, "I was wrong – I really have not forgiven you after all." But if I have shown you mercy, this has been done – once and for all. Also, with respect to mercy, it is not necessary that I – in showing it – must be the one wronged or injured by your wrongful conduct. (It is not even necessary that anyone be wronged.) All that is required is that you stand under certain rules and that I have authority to treat you in a certain harsh way because of those rules. But the matter is different with forgiveness. To use a legal term, I do not have *standing* to resent or forgive you unless I have myself been the victim of your wrongdoing. I may forgive you for embezzling my funds; but it would be ludicrous for me, for example, to claim that I had decided to forgive Hitler for what he did to the Jews. I lack the proper standing for this. Thus, I may legitimately resent (and hence consider forgiving) only wrong done *to me*.[9] If I forgive, this will primarily be a matter of my forswearing my resentment toward the person who has wronged me – a change of attitude quite compatible with my still demanding certain harsh public consequences for the wrongdoer. My forgiving you for embezzling my funds is not, for example, incompatible with a demand that you return my funds or even with a demand that you suffer just legal punishment for what you have done. Neither does

---

9 In "Rebellion" (Dostoevsky, *The Brothers Karamazov*), Ivan considers the suffering of innocents – especially children – and is outraged at the thought that anyone except the children (or perhaps their mothers) could forgive the injuries suffered.

Sometimes, of course, I will psychologically identify with some persons and will see injuries to them as in some sense injuries to me. I may feel this way, for example, about my children. Here resentment does have a life. There is enormous individual variation, of course, in the degree to which people are psychologically identified with others – even strangers.

my forgiveness entail that I must trust you with my money in the future. Forgiveness restores moral equality but not necessarily equality in every respect – for example, equality of trust. Some harsh treatment would, of course, be incompatible with forgiveness – namely, harsh treatment the very point of which would be to show you how much I hate and resent you. But when the harsh treatment is based on other factors (e.g., a concern with legal justice), forgiveness need pose no obstacle to such treatment.

Having become clearer on what forgiveness is not, let us return to Butler's account of what it is: the forswearing of resentment. Butler's puzzle was this: How could a loving God who commanded that we love our neighbor implant in us so unloving a passion as resentment? Is not this attitude unambiguously bad and any actions or practices based on it (retributive punishment perhaps) also bad? In answering *no* to this question, Butler suggests that resentment understandably arouses suspicion because it is often inappropriate (e.g., directed toward trivial affronts instead of real injuries) and sometimes provokes excessive behavior (e.g., vigilante activity). As Butler sees, however, it would be a mistake to condemn a passion simply because it admits of pathological or irrational extensions. (What passion does not?) Resentment expresses respect for the demands of morality (particularly, as I have argued, for the demands for *self-respect*) and is thus – when so described – consistent, in Butler's view, with any reasonable interpretation of a gospel of love. (Butler has no patience with attempts to view the Christian ethic as irrational sentimentality.) What is not consistent with a gospel of love is being dominated by the passion of resentment or acting unjustly on the basis of that passion; and thus Butler sees forgiveness as a virtue that functions to check resentment and keep it within proper bounds.

Is forgiveness then nothing but the overcoming (or attempt at overcoming) of resentment? Is every instance where resentment is overcome a case of the virtue of forgiveness? I (agreeing, I believe, with Butler) think not; and two sorts of cases will aid in establishing this negative answer. First, consider the case of *forgetting*. Sometimes we lose a vivid memory of old wrongs, become bored with our resentments, and simply forget. But this just *happens* to us; that is, it is totally non-voluntary. As such, it seems too removed from agency to count as a moral virtue – though it still might be a desirable disposition of character to possess. Thus, to the extent that forgiveness is properly regarded as a moral virtue, it strikes me as a mistake to identify forgiving with forgetting. We tend to use the phrase "forgive and forget," and I do not believe the phrase is redundant.[10]   ← bot forgiveness

Or consider this second case: You have wronged me deeply, and I deeply resent you for it. The resentment eats away at my peace of mind – I lose sleep, snap at my friends, become less effective at my work, and so on. In short, my resentment so dominates my mental life that I am being made miserable. In order to regain my peace of mind, I go to a behavior-modification therapist to have my resentment extinguished. (Let us suppose there are such techniques.) Have I forgiven you? Surely not – at least not in any sense where forgiveness is supposed to be a moral virtue. For my motivation here was not moral at all; it was purely *selfish*: the desire to promote my own mental health.

What is starting to emerge from this discussion is this: The question "What is forgiveness?" cannot after all be sharply distinguished from the question "How is forgiveness justified?" As the foregoing cases show, not all instances of ceasing to resent will be ones of forgiveness – for example, forgetting is not. We cannot define forgiveness and *then* ask what moral reasons make it appropriate; because, I suggest, my ceasing to resent will not constitute forgiveness unless it is

10 Although I am not here able to pursue the matter in any depth, I should at least note that forgetting is in fact more complex than this account suggests. As both Nietzsche and Freud have taught us, some cases that appear to involve mere non-voluntary forgetting might, when analyzed in depth, prove to be complex (though unconscious) rational strategies – strategies for which an individual might legitimately be held accountable. Here cases that initially look like mere forgetting might merit reclassification as forgetting of a more complex sort or even as forgiving.

done for a moral reason. Forgiveness is not the overcoming of resentment *simpliciter*; it is rather this: forswearing resentment on moral grounds.

What, then, are the moral grounds; that is, what sorts of reasons justify or at least render appropriate an act of forgiveness? Let me start to answer this question simply by listing five reasons that are, in ordinary life and discourse, those most often given as grounds for forgiveness. We will then consider if this is just a laundry list or if some rational principle unites them or some set of them. The reasons are these:

I will forgive the person who has willfully wronged me, because

1. he repented or had a change of heart *or*
2. he meant well (his motives were good)[11] *or*
3. he has suffered enough *or*
4. he has undergone humiliation (perhaps some ritual humiliation, e.g., the apology ritual of "I beg forgiveness") *or*
5. of old times' sake (e.g., "He has been a good and loyal friend to me in the past").

Let me say something about what these reasons tend to have in common and then say something in detail about each one. But first recall the background here: Acceptable grounds for forgiveness must be compatible with self-respect, respect for others as moral agents, and respect for the rules of morality or the moral order. Can forgiveness ever be consistent with such constraints? I think that it can be for cases where we can draw a distinction between the immoral *act* and the immoral *agent*; for then we can follow Saint Augustine's counsel and "hate the sin but not the sinner." It is, of course, impossible to hate the sin and not the sinner if the sinner is intimately identified with his sin - if the wrongdoer is intimately identified with his wrongdoing. But to the extent that the agent is separated from his evil act, forgiveness *of him* is

11 This point is stressed by Elizabeth Beardsley in her "Understanding and Forgiveness" in *The Philosophy of Brand Blanshard*, ed. Paul Arthur Schilpp (La Salle, Ill.: Open Court, 1981).

possible without a tacit approval of his evil act. A similar divorce of act from agent will also help to square forgiveness with self-respect. One reason we so deeply resent moral injuries done to us is not simply that they hurt us in some tangible or sensible way; it is because such injuries are also *messages* – symbolic communications. They are ways a wrongdoer has of saying to us, "I count but you do not," "I can use you for my purposes," or "I am here up high and you are there down below." Intentional wrongdoing *insults* us and attempts (sometimes successfully) to *degrade* us – and thus it involves a kind of injury that is not merely tangible and sensible. It is moral injury, and we care about such injuries. (As Justice Holmes observed, even a dog notices and cares about the difference between being tripped over accidentally and being kicked intentionally.) Most of us tend to care about what others (at least *some* others, some significant group whose good opinion we value) think about us – how much they think we matter. Our self-respect is *social* in at least this sense, and it is simply part of the human condition that we are weak and vulnerable in these ways. And thus when we are treated with contempt by others it attacks us in profound and deeply threatening ways. We resent (or worse) those who so attack us, and want to separate ourselves from them – to harm them in turn or at least to banish them from the realm of those whose well-being should be our concern.

But what if they come to separate or divorce themselves from their own evil act? (True repentance is a clear way of doing this.) Then the insulting message is no longer present – no longer endorsed by the wrongdoer. We can then join the wrongdoer in condemning the very act from which he now stands emotionally separated. Thus to the degree that the items on the preceding list represent ways in which an agent can be divorced from his evil act, they represent grounds for forgiveness that are compatible with self-respect and respect for the rules of the moral order. To explore this idea of "divorce of act from agent," let us now look a bit more closely at each of the five listed reasons.

25

1. *Repentance.* This is surely the clearest way in which a wrongdoer can sever himself from his past wrong. In having a sincere change of heart, he is withdrawing his endorsement from his own immoral past behavior; he is saying, "I no longer stand behind the wrongdoing, and I want to be separated from it. I stand with you in condemning it." Of such a person it cannot be said that he is *now* conveying the message that he holds me in contempt. Thus I can relate to him now, through forgiveness, without fearing my own acquiescence in immorality or in judgments that I lack worth. I forgive him for what he now is.

2. *Good motives.* Sometimes people wrong us without meaning to convey that they hold us in contempt or think we are of less worth than they are. Paternalism is a good example to illustrate this point. A person who interferes with my liberty for what he thinks is my own good is, in my judgment, acting wrongly; that is, he is interfering in my "moral space" in a way he has no right to. His grounds for interfering, however, are well meaning (i.e., he seeks to do me good) even if his actions are misguided and morally insensitive. (Perhaps he is overattentive to utilitarian considerations at the expense of considerations of rights and justice.) It is hard to view the friend who locks my liquor cabinet because he knows I drink too much as on exactly the same moral level as the person who embezzles my funds for his own benefit – even though both are violating my rights. Thus the case for forgiving the former (at least the first time) strikes me as having some merit.

3. *Enough suffering.* The claim "He has suffered enough" as grounds for forgiveness may understandably be viewed with suspicion; for example, we may think it was involved in such controversial events as President Gerald Ford's pardon of Richard Nixon on the grounds that Nixon, disgraced and forced to resign as president, had suffered enough. But two cautions are relevant here. First, Nixon was not simply forgiven (if he was forgiven at all); he was treated with *mercy.* To

pardon someone is not to change the way one feels about him but is to let him avoid what may well be his just deserts. Second, just because *some* suffering may be relevant to forgiveness, it does not follow that *any* suffering is. The suffering occasioned by falling from a position that (as one's wrongful actions demonstrate) one had no right to occupy in the first place hardly seems relevant from the moral point of view.[12]

But what would relevant suffering be? I am not sure, actually, and some part of me wants to throw this consideration out entirely as simply confusion or even superstition. And yet some other part of me cannot quite do this. There is the thought, widespread in our culture, that *suffering is redemptive.* (One thinks, for example, of the old Oedipus in *Oedipus at Colonus.*) This connection between suffering and redemption could, of course, simply be a kind of empirical claim – e.g., the claim that suffering tends to provoke repentance. If so, then the intelligible content of "He has suffered enough" is redundant, collapsing into point 1 above. So too if the suffering is simply guilt or other pangs of conscience. Perhaps there is something in this thought: Wrongdoers attempt to *degrade* us, to bring us low – lower than themselves. We will find it difficult to forgive and restore relations with them in this posture without acquiescing in our own lowered status – something that any self-respecting person is loath to do. But suffering tends to bring people low, to reduce them, to humble them. If so, then enough equality may be restored in order to forgive them consistent with self-respect. They may not have severed themselves from their own evil acts, but there is perhaps a sense in which they have been severed.

12 See *U.S. v. Bergman*, United States District Court, S.D.N.Y., 1976, 416 F. Supp. 496. Rabbi Bergman was convicted of criminal fraud in connection with the operation of some of his nursing homes. He tried to avoid a prison sentence by arguing that he had been disgraced and had thus suffered enough. Judge Frankel was underwhelmed by this argument and suggested that, as Bergman's crimes demonstrated, he was "suffering from loss of public esteem . . . that had been, at least in some measure, wrongly bestowed and enjoyed."

Given the hurt and sadness that may come to be present in a person's life, it may be difficult and improper to retain, as one's *primary* view of that person, the sense that he is essentially "the one who has wronged me." Perhaps he does and should become in one's mind simply "that poor bastard."

4. *Humiliation*. What I want to say about humiliation continues the preceding thought about suffering and involves the role of *ritual* in our moral life. We tend to think that rituals are practices that primitive savages have, and that we civilized folks have outgrown this sort of thing. But we are deeply mistaken when we think this. Philosophers have not, I think, paid sufficient attention to the role of ritual in moral relations – a role that illuminates certain aspects of forgiveness.[13] As I mentioned before, wrongdoers attempt (sometimes successfully) to degrade or insult us; to bring us low; to say, "I am on high while you are down there below." As a result, we in a real sense *lose face* when done a moral injury – one reason why easy forgiveness tends to compromise self-esteem. But our moral relations provide for a ritual whereby the wrongdoer can symbolically bring himself low (or raise us up – I am not sure which metaphor best captures the point) – in other words, the humbling ritual of *apology*, the language of which is often that of *begging* for forgiveness. The posture of begging is not very exalted, of course, and thus some symbolic equality – necessary if forgiveness is to proceed consistently with self-respect – is now present. Sometimes, of course, the apology is more than mere ritual; indeed, in the best of cases it is likely to be a way of manifesting repentance. Here it will collapse into point 1. At other times we will settle simply for the ritual – so long as it is not transparently insincere.[14]

13 One philosopher who has appreciated the role of ritual in our moral life is Gareth Matthews. See his "Ritual and the Religious Feelings," in *Explaining Emotions*, ed. Amelie Oksenberg Rorty (Berkeley: University of California Press, 1980), pp. 339–53.

14 On the role of humiliation ("humbling of the will"), see Herbert Fingarette's presidential address in *Proceedings of the American Philosophical Association*, 1977.

5. Old times' sake. As with repentance, we have here a clear case of divorce of act from agent. When you are repentant, I forgive you for what you *now* are. When I forgive you for old times' sake, I forgive you for what you *once were*. Much of our forgiveness of old friends and parents, for example, is of this sort.

The upshot of what I have argued thus far is this: Forgiveness of a wrongdoer on the basis of any of the preceding grounds (grounds which in various ways divorce act from agent) may be consistent with self-respect, respect for others, and respect for the rules of the moral order. All this shows, of course, is that forgiveness - when directed (for example) toward a truly repentant wrongdoer - is permissible, not wrong because not inconsistent with self-respect. But if forgiveness is a virtue, then it must be that sometimes it is not merely permissible that I forgive but that I *ought* to forgive and can be properly criticized if I do not. Perhaps nobody has a *right* to be forgiven (imposing on others a perfect duty to forgive him), but surely forgiveness - if a virtue - must be like charity in at least this way: Just as charity requires that I sometimes ought to assist those having no right to my assistance, so does forgiveness require that I sometimes ought to forgive those having no right to my forgiveness.

How might one argue for this stronger view? One argument has been latent in what I have said thus far. Although repentance does not give one a right to be forgiven, there is a sense in which it may make resentment *inappropriate* - for why should I resent you now for holding me in contempt when your sincere repentance makes it clear that you do not now hold me in contempt? There is a clear sense in which it is simply not *rational* to continue holding attitudes when I have come to see their inappropriateness and thus - as a rational being - I ought to forswear those attitudes. Just as rational beings value true beliefs, so they should, I think, value appropriate attitudes - attitudes fitting to their objects. This is why rational beings will seek to root out such things as phobias and other neurotic emotions from their psychologies; and so too, I should think, for inappropriate attitudes of resentment. This then is one argument for why we sometimes *ought* to forgive others – why forgiveness is sometimes more than merely permissible, why forgiveness is – in short – sometimes a virtue.

But there are other arguments as well. Two of them I associate particularly with the Christian tradition; and, since neither relies on the divorce between act and agent that I have made central, it will be worth exploring them briefly to see if they add a significant new dimension to the understanding of forgiveness. The arguments are these:

1. We should forgive in order to reform the wrongdoer; i.e., we should forgive, not because the wrongdoer has repented, but as a step toward bringing his repentance about, making it at least easier for him.
2. We should forgive because we ourselves need to be forgiven. (This, I take it, is the point of the parable of the unforgiving servant in Matt. 18:21–35.)

These grounds for forgiveness may be what prompted Feuerbach and others to suggest that forgiveness cannot be accounted for in ordinary moral and secular terms – that it takes us beyond morality and into a religious dimension that transcends or suspends the ordinarily ethical.[15] I know that some people value obscurity and mystery for their own sake, but I am myself inclined to resist these leaps into special realms. Sometimes we can mine these religious traditions for nuggets of secular value – i.e., values we can recognize even if we do not accept the theological views in which they were originally embedded. Thus we can sometimes avoid leaps into the mysterious and edifying if we will simply think about the matter a bit more. Point 1 above, for example, could be a kind of empirical prediction – almost therapeutic in nature – about what is likely to produce repentance and

15 For a discussion of Feuerbach and others on this matter, see Chapter 6 of Allen Wood's *Kant's Moral Religion* (Ithaca, N.Y.: Cornell University Press, 1970).

WILLIAMS SUCKS

reform; and, as such, this ground for forgiveness is surely compatible with one's own self-respect. Less clear, however, is the degree to which it is compatible with respect for the wrongdoer. Suppose you had wronged someone. How would you like it if that person assumed that you could not come to repentance on your own but required the aid of his ministry of forgiveness? Might you not feel patronized – condescended to? Forgiveness can be an act of weakness, but it can also be an act of arrogance. Seeing it this way, the wrongdoer might well resent the forgiveness. "Who do you think you are to forgive me?" he might respond to such well-meaning meddling.

But what about point 2 – the need we all have for being forgiven? Recall the parable of the unforgiving servant: A lord had decided to punish and generally ruin his servant's life because that servant had not paid a debt that he owed to the lord. The servant prostrated himself and begged piteously, however, and the lord was moved by compassion and forgave him his debt. Shortly after this, that very servant called in a debt owed to him by one of his underlings. He was unmoved by the pleas of his debtor, however. He refused to forgive the debt and consigned his debtor to prison. The lord, learning of this, called the servant in. Telling the servant that he should have showed compassion comparable to the compassion he received, the lord withdrew his forgiveness of the servant and "delivered him to the tormentors." Jesus concludes the parable by saying: "So likewise shall my heavenly Father do also unto you, if ye from your hearts forgive not every one his brother their trespasses."

What exactly is the argument in favor of forgiveness that is being given here? On one interpretation, the whole appeal looks pretty dreadful – of the kind that Nietzsche liked to note when arguing that Christianity is simply sublimated *ressentiment*. For on the surface the parable looks like nothing but an appeal to our baser instincts of *fear*: If you do not forgive others, then God will not forgive you and then you are in for it. One might reject this appeal either because one does not believe in God or because one will try to resist, on

31

grounds of moral integrity, being bullied by appeals to one's lesser nature. How, in short, can an act of forgiveness exemplify a moral virtue if it is motivated simply by a fear of what some supernatural sorehead will do if one fails to forgive?[16]

But such a rejection would, I think, be too quick. As is often the case with religious parables, there is deep moral insight waiting to be discovered if one will simply explore them with some patience. And the insight in the present parable (which can surely be granted by the most secular or even atheistic reader) is to be seen in its character as a parable on *moral humility*. Each of us, if honest, will admit two things about ourselves: (1) We will within the course of our lives wrong others – even others about whom we care deeply; and (2) because we care so deeply about these others and our relationships with them, we will want to be forgiven by them for our wrongdoings. In this sense we do all need and desire forgiveness and would not want to live in a world where the disposition to forgive was not present and regarded as a healing and restoring virtue. Given that this is the sort of world we all need and want, is it not then incumbent upon each of us to cultivate the disposition to forgive – not the flabby sentimentality of forgiving every wrong, no matter how deep or unrepented, but at least the willingness to be open to the possibility of forgiveness with hope and some trust? Only a person so arrogant as to believe that he will never wrong others or need to be forgiven by them could (in Kantian language) consistently will membership in a world without forgiveness. To see that none of us is such a person is a lesson in moral humility and is, at least in part, the message of the parable.

Suppose one accepts all of this. To what degree can the virtue of forgiveness, so conceived, be relevant to the law? It

16 For an argument that this characterization of the response to divine commands may be superficial, see my "Kantian Autonomy and Divine Commands," *Faith and Philosophy*, 4 (July 1987), pp. 276–81. See also Peter Geach's "The Moral Law and the Law of God" in his collection of essays *God and the Soul* (London: Routledge & Kegan Paul, 1969).

surely has at least this relevance: To the degree that Stephen is correct in his view that the law institutionalizes resentment, then to that same degree the law has a reason to go easy on those persons who have been forgiven or for whom forgiveness is appropriate. To the degree that the law does more than institutionalize resentment, however, forgiveness is without relevance to legal response. And surely the law does more – considerably more – than merely institutionalize resentment. As Hobbes taught us, for example, law functions to maintain obedience to rules without which civilized life would be impossible; and if one believed that the punishment of an individual was required to maintain these rules, one could consistently advocate such punishment even if one had forgiven the individual to be punished. To forgive a wrongdoer involves a change of heart toward that person (the overcoming of resentment toward him), but this is not necessarily a change in one's view on how that wrongdoer is to be treated. Because I have ceased to hate the person who has wronged me it does not follow that I act inconsistently if I still advocate his being forced to pay compensation for the harm he has done or his being forced to undergo punishment for his wrongdoing – that he, in short, get his just deserts.[17]

The arena of resentment and forgiveness is individual and personal in a way that legal guilt and responsibility are not. I have the proper standing to forgive injuries done to me, but

17 Why, then, should the beneficiary of forgiveness care that he is forgiven if he must still face harsh consequences? Surely he will care for the same reason that the victim of his original injustice cared about the intangible harm he received. Normal human beings, in normal human relations, simply care deeply about the attitudes that (some) other people have toward them – about the messages of respect or lack of respect that are conveyed. Thus most of us can easily imagine a case where, although repentant, we are justly punished yet forgiven (even loved) and another case where we are justly punished and not forgiven (even hated). The punishment will hurt the same in both cases, and yet who would not prefer the former to the latter? Recall Melville's *Billy Budd* and how deeply both Billy and Captain Vere cared – independently of the legal consequences that each knew were inevitable – about how each *felt* about the other. Is there anything at all puzzling about this?

I do not have the proper standing to let people off the hook for all of their legal accountability. To do the latter is to show *mercy* and is necessarily to *act* (and not just to feel) in a certain way. Forgiveness and mercy are often confused, but they should not be. (Some of Butler's remarks about the social and legal dimensions of forgiveness, for example, might more clearly apply to the topic of mercy.) There is a sense, however, in which mercy may be the legal analogue of forgiveness with this difference: Forgiveness involves the *overcoming* of certain passions (resentment, hatred) when they are inappropriate, whereas mercy involves acting in a certain way *because* of certain passions (love, compassion). Both may be virtues, but they are different virtues and operate in different sorts of context — a topic to be explored in more detail in Chapter 5.

Chapter 2

Forgiveness, resentment and hatred

JEAN HAMPTON

Sir Joshua told us a curious particular of Dr. Adam
Smith. He had taken a resolution that he would hate
nobody, and if he knew himself, there was nobody in
the world whom he hated. This was a new thought to
me for the moment, and I am afraid it is new to most
people in actual *practice*. But it is an essential principle
of Christianity. Let me try it. But it does not exclude
a certain degree of aversion to some compared to others.

James Boswell, *Journal*, February 23, 1788

We are constantly exhorted to forgive those who wrong us.
However, in Chapter 1[1] Jeffrie Murphy is sympathetic to the
Nietzschean thought that forgiveness may, at least in certain
circumstances, be harmful and wrong, a vice rather than a
virtue. Like Bishop Butler, Murphy understands forgiveness
as the overcoming of resentment. But the failure to resent a
moral injury need not be a good thing: "If I count morally as
much as anyone else (as surely I do), a failure to resent moral
injuries done to me is a failure to care about the moral value
incarnate in my own person (that I am, in Kantian language,
an end in myself) and thus a failure to care about the very
rules of morality."[2] So we face the following puzzle: how can

— Murphy

1 And in Murphy's "Forgiveness and Resentment," in *Minnesota Studies
in Philosophy*, Vol. VII, *Social and Political Philosophy*, ed. Peter A.
French, Theodore E. Uehling, Jr., and Howard R. Wettstein
(Minneapolis: University of Minnesota Press, 1982), pp. 503–16.
2 Murphy, Chapter 1 of the present volume.

forgiveness be a duty when it seems to involve overcoming a useful, even therapeutic emotion in a way that can do harm to the forgiver? Murphy's solution to the puzzle, namely, that at times it is *not* a duty, may unnerve many of us. Is he right?

I. THE DEFINITION OF FORGIVENESS

Murphy's puzzle naturally arises from his and Butler's understanding of forgiveness as the "overcoming of resentment." If that definition is not correct, then the problem of determining the moral appropriateness of forgiveness might need a different formulation, and thus admit of a different answer, than that given by Murphy. So in true Socratic fashion, I want to preface a discussion of when (if ever) we should forgive our wrongdoers by asking what forgiveness is and, in the process, reconsidering Murphy's definition of it.

Murphy himself is dissatisfied with the definition of forgiveness as the overcoming of resentment because he thinks it is incomplete. We do not, he says, think someone has forgiven a wrongdoer if he overcomes his resentment towards her by simply forgetting the crime she committed against him or by taking behavior-modification therapy to extinguish it. So Murphy adds that forgiveness is, more precisely, the overcoming of anger towards one's wrongdoer for moral reasons.

But this emendation doesn't seem to be enough to fix the definition, because we typically think of forgiveness as an act which is "directed" at the wrongdoer, and not merely as some kind of internal emotional change inside the victim. If, for example, a victim overcame resentment towards his wrongdoer for moral reasons (e.g., because he believed that festering resentment affected his ability to respond lovingly to other human beings), yet sustained the belief (held soberly, and not in anger) that his wrongdoer was a terrible person and one with whom he should not associate, we would not say that he had forgiven his wrongdoer, only that he was no longer angry at her. So forgiveness must be defined so that it involves more than simply effecting certain psychological changes for moral reasons. Of course it may presuppose such changes in order to be possible, but it is a response that is centrally concerned with the forgiver's relationship to the wrongdoer. Thus we speak of forgiveness as "bestowed upon" or "offered to" the wrongdoer.

Is the biblical approach to characterizing forgiveness more successful than Murphy's or Butler's approach? Consider the Hebrew words used in the Old Testament to refer to forgiveness. The words *kipper* meaning "to cover," *nasa* meaning "to lift up, or carry away," and *salach* probably meaning "to let go" are all used to describe forgiveness; and they are each, in different ways, metaphors for the forgiver's removal of sin from the wrongdoer.[3] Forgiveness is understood as "covering" the sin so that each party can approach the other without the sin in full view. It also "carries away" the wrongdoing, thereby cleansing the person who committed it. The one who has been wronged "lets go" of her victimization, of her sense of having been wronged by the other. Similarly, in the New Testament the Greek verb *aphiemi* is used in the presentations of Jesus' concept of forgiveness, and this word can mean "to remit, send away, or liberate" as well as "to forgive."[4] These ways of speaking suggest that when the wrongdoer is forgiven, it is presumed that he has committed an immoral action, but the forgiver nonetheless "forgets" what the wrongdoer has done to him, not literally, but in the sense that he will not let the wrongdoing continue to intrude into his dealings with the wrongdoer in order that they can reestablish some kind of relationship – at the very least, the "civil" relationship that prevails between strangers in a human community.

Jesus sometimes speaks of forgiving not only people but also actions, where the latter is specifically compared to the absolving of a debt. But forgiving an action is preparatory to

---

3 See the entry under forgiveness in *A Theological Word Book of the Bible*, ed. Alan Richardson (New York: Macmillan, 1951).
4 John Howard Yoder discusses this in *The Politics of Jesus* (Grand Rapids, Mich.: Eerdmans, 1972), p. 66.

the forgiveness of the wrongdoer. When the victim "sends away" the immoral action in the way that a creditor would absolve a debt, he no longer holds the immoral action against the wrongdoer (in the same way that a creditor would no longer hold the debt against the debtor). By removing it, the forgiver is able to respond to the wrongdoer as someone other than "the one who hurt me," and the wrongdoer himself is able, thanks to this new perspective, to regard himself as liberated from his burden of moral debt. Such liberation puts the two parties on an equal footing once more, and makes possible renewed relationships.[5]

So this metaphoric language assumes that forgiveness involves overcoming a *point of view*, namely, the point of view of the other as "the one who wronged me." This point of view is the product of a judgement of the other as one's transgressor, so it seems that it is really *this* judgement which a victim must "let go of" if he is going to be able to welcome that person back into his life.

Murphy's and Butler's definition of forgiveness as the overcoming of resentment may not be substantially different, however, from this biblical definition if one accepts (as Murphy does) a cognitive understanding of resentment. As Murphy describes it, that emotion essentially carries within it the judgement of the action as wrong, and thus the judgement of its perpetrator as a wrongdoer (assuming that the agent's performance of it cannot be excused). He might contend that overcoming resentment necessarily involves overcoming the latter judgement, and not merely overcoming the angry feeling that tends to accompany that judgement. So overcoming both, he could argue, is central to the act of forgiving.

Suppose we understand Murphy's definition in this way. I want to argue that it is still not good enough, because there

5 Herbert Morris discusses a way in which one can literally see wrongdoers as "debtors" of a kind in his "Persons and Punishment," in *Punishment and Rehabilitation*, ed. J. Murphy (Belmont, Calif.: Wadsworth, 1985); originally published in *The Monist*, 52 (October 1968), pp. 475–501. I shall criticize Morris's view in Chapter 4.

38

is a way of overcoming one's angry feelings towards a
wrongdoer, dropping one's judgement of him as a wrongdoer, and even doing so for moral reasons, which still fails to
be forgiveness. To illustrate this non-forgiving response,
consider the following case of family conflict: A woman mar-
ries a man with a stern, rather rigid father who is getting on
in years. The father comes to stay with the couple for a visit,
and finds his daughter-in-law's conduct irritating, the food
less than perfect, the house less than clean, the conversation
rather dull; in small ways he makes his dissatisfaction
known, and he also makes it clear that he considers the
daughter-in-law to blame for the imperfections in his son's
house. Whatever the motivations for the old man's attacks,
let us suppose that they are unfair and give pain to the
daughter-in-law. However, her husband says to her: "Look,
he is my father and we should be on good terms with him.
I know you think he is behaving badly, but be good and forgive him so that family peace can be preserved."

I would argue that the husband is not really requesting his
wife to engage in genuine "forgiveness" towards the father-
in-law. Resentment of the father-in-law's bad behavior is reasonable given that his behavior is genuinely wrong, but the
husband is asking his wife to "drop" that judgement and the
angry feelings it engenders, and go on to respond to the
father-in-law as if no offense had occurred, for the sake of
preserving harmony in the family. If the daughter-in-law
were to "overcome" her resentment in this sense, that is, to
"repudiate and drive out" that emotion, she would not only
be allowing someone to continue to injure her but also preparing herself to condone that injury for the sake of an end
which at least appears moral (family peace) and which is supposed to be more important than securing the recognition
that she has been injured. Aurel Kolnai rightly distinguishes
forgiveness from this sort of dangerous response to others'
wrongdoing, which he calls "condonation."[6] Those who

6 See Kolnai's "Forgiveness," *Proceedings of the Aristotelian Society*,
1973–4, pp. 91–106.

continually engage in such condonation risk undermining their sense of self-worth and becoming servile to others. I will define 'condonation' as the acceptance, without moral protest (either inward or outward), of an action which ought to warrant such protest, made possible, first, by ridding oneself of the judgement that the action is wrong, so that its performer cannot be a wrongdoer, and, second, by ridding oneself of any attendant feelings (such as those which are involved in resentment) which signify one's protest of the action.

Condonation might be possible only if one engages in self-deception, telling oneself the lie that the immoral action is not immoral after all. If so, I am skeptical about how often one is able to do it. Lying to oneself about a wrong may not be a very good way of getting oneself to believe that it wasn't a wrong. Still, even if it involves self-deception, I wonder if attempting it isn't, nonetheless, sometimes morally appropriate.[7] Life with relatives, roommates, spouses and colleagues may demand of us this "moral compromise" on occasion, because insisting on our rights in the face of moral injury on every occasion can itself be harmful to maintaining good relationships with them. Indeed, avoiding a dangerous anger towards oneself may sometimes require one to turn a blind eye to one's own moral faults.

But condonation is not forgiveness. The central difference between them is that condonation involves accepting the moral wrong whereas forgiveness does not.[8] Forgiving someone presupposes that the action to be forgiven *was* wrong, and nothing in the act of forgiveness communicates to the wrongdoer that her action was permissible after all, or that the forgiver has decided to reject as inappropriate any previous resentment of it. Nietzsche had some sense of this when he charged that forgiveness could be a very arrogant act. One who is forgiven for behavior which she does not

7 So does Kolnai; see ibid., p. 96.
8 Kolnai makes a similar point; see ibid., pp. 96–7.

believe was wrong tends to regard the forgiveness as an affront, a patronizing and insulting gesture, just as an innocent person will take offense at being granted a pardon for a crime she didn't commit. And this is because those who forgive or pardon wrongdoers do not intend to make statements to the effect that the wrongdoing never really existed; instead the wrongdoers are told that the forgiveness or the pardon is offered *for* the wrongdoing. But if forgivers never give up the idea that the action was wrong, how can they ever give up the view of the actor as a wrongdoer?

This question, generated by the realization that not every kind of morally motivated overcoming of the judgement of another as a wrongdoer counts as forgiveness, can be made part of an argument that threatens to undermine the concept of forgiveness entirely. If we insist that forgiveness is a response to a wrong that is distinguished from condonation, then how can it still be a way of absolving the wrongdoer from guilt? How can you absolve someone from guilt and still remain committed to the idea that his actions were wrong and unacceptable? Perhaps such commitment can occur along with absolution if, but only if, the wrongdoer has previously repented of his crime. But if you now renew a relationship with him, it is unclear that you have forgiven him. Before his repentance you were morally required to sever any dealings with him, on the grounds that he had behaved immorally; but doesn't his repentance morally oblige you to reaccept him on the grounds that he has now become a person who has repudiated the action and who thus merits moral respect? Isn't such reacceptance the fair or just thing to do? Anyone who acts on the principle "Hate and avoid those who are committed to immoral behavior; love and respect those who despise moral behavior" would renew relations with a repentant person in just the way that the advocate of forgiveness would require, and would do so in circumstances that make it clear that she is not condoning the offense, but curiously *she would not be forgiving him.* She would merely be treating him fairly, justly, reasonably, in view of his change of heart. So, to insist that renewed relations take place only

41

in circumstances that preclude anyone from interpreting the renewal as the condonation of the wrongdoer's act seems to render forgiveness unnecessary, a redundant act.

For Aurel Kolnai this is the paradox of forgiveness. The paradox can be stated in a nutshell as follows: What seems required to make a change of heart towards a wrongdoer something other than condonation supplies the foundation for explaining and justifying that change of heart as something other than forgiveness. The paradox might move some to conclude that the concept of forgiveness is internally incoherent, so that one who commends it is speaking either of condonation or of the practice of valuing others in accordance with their virtue.

But if forgiveness is going to be "salvaged from logical havoc" as Kolnai puts it, one needs to determine how it is possible for one who has been wronged to forgive *something* in the wrongdoer, that is, to absolve a genuine and subsisting guilt in him, without that practice becoming, to all intents and purposes, a condonation of his immoral action or the immoral character traits he has displayed in performing the action. Definitions of forgiveness as the "overcoming of resentment for moral reasons" or the "overcoming of the judgement of another as a wrongdoer for moral reasons" are at best incomplete because neither tells us enough about what forgiveness is to enable us to solve this paradox.

In this chapter I will try to develop a definition that will allow us to solve the paradox, in preparation for my argument (in Chapter 4) that forgiveness is a morally impressive response to wrongdoers that is much less problematic than Murphy thinks. But the going must be slow. The preceding remarks already suggest that forgiveness should be analyzed as a *process* involving, not only certain psychological preparations (mainly the overcoming of various forms of anger) but, more positively, a change of heart towards the wrongdoer which is something other than a condoning of her action and which is normally accompanied by an offer of reconciliation.[9]

9 Note that this reconciliation need not be made in words (we have a vari-

Murphy's use of the word 'forgiveness' generally refers not to this complicated process but to that portion of the process which I have called the change of heart, and this seems to respect common linguistic practice. But he and Butler (and the authors of various books of the Bible) try to characterize that change of heart by focusing on what the forgiver must overcome in order to have it. The paradox shows that this approach fails because the essence of forgiveness remains uncaptured. I want to pursue directly what that change of heart is.

Nonetheless, I will start that pursuit by discussing in detail the psychological preparations required for this change of heart to occur. By specifying exactly what one who would forgive must "let go of," I hope to clear the way for a proper definition of the positive action which such preparations make possible. I will look at a number of emotional and psychological responses to wrongdoings which victims experience, and will try to describe what I see (and have felt) these responses to be. The territory I will travel has been relatively untravelled by philosophers, so the terms and the structures I have developed to describe the phenomena are largely my own. The discussion attempts to answer to no philosophical theory in ethics, but only to the phenomena themselves.

II. BEING INSULTED AND BEING DEGRADED

What is it that really bothers us about being wronged? It is not simply that wrongdoings threaten or produce physical or psychological damage, or damage to our careers, interests or families. However much we may sorrow over our bad for-

---

ety of ways of welcoming someone back). Forgiveness can also take place without reconciliation: an offer may be impossible (e.g., if the wrongdoer has died) or morally unwise (e.g., if renewing the relationship might inadvertently encourage more wrongdoing) and yet forgiveness of the wrongdoing can still occur. But generally, one who is supposed to have experienced a "change of heart" towards a wrongdoer but who still finds the prospect of associating with the wrongdoer disturbing has probably not succeeded in forgiving the wrongdoer.

tune, when the same damage is threatened or produced by natural forces or by accidents, we do not experience that special anger that comes from having been *insulted.* When someone wrongs another, she does not regard her victim as the sort of person who is valuable enough to require better treatment. Whereas nature cannot treat us in accord with our moral value, (we believe other human beings are able and required to do so.) Hence, when they do not, we are insulted in the sense that we believe they have ignored the high standing that value gives us. As Murphy notes:

> One reason we so deeply resent moral injuries done to us is not simply that they hurt us in some tangible or sensible way; it is because such injuries are also *messages* – symbolic communications. They are ways a wrongdoer has of saying to us, "I count but you do not," "I can use you for my purposes," or "I am here up high and you are there down below." Intentional wrongdoing *insults* us and attempts (sometimes successfully) to degrade us – and thus it involves a kind of injury that is not merely tangible and sensible. It is moral injury, and we care about such injuries.[10]

But there is more than one way of being "lowered," and thus more than one kind of moral injury.

Consider Murphy's characterization of the message sent by the wrongdoer to his victim; the wrongdoer is saying that she is not *worth* enough for him to accord her better treatment. Now there are (at least) the following two ways a victim can respond to this message: She can reject it as wrong and hence regard the action as inappropriate given what she believes to be her true (high) worth, or she can worry (or even believe) that the wrongdoer is right, that she really isn't worth enough to warrant better treatment, so that his action is permissible given her lower worth.

If she responds in the first way, she perceives herself to have suffered *no literal degradation* as a result of the wrongdoing. Her high value is, she believes, unchanged despite the

10 See Chapter 1.

action. But she is nonetheless *demeaned* in the sense that she has been forced to endure treatment that is too low for her. So there is a difference between being demeaned and being literally lowered in value. A prince who is mistaken for a pauper and who therefore fails to receive royal treatment will regard this treatment as demeaning, not because he will believe or even worry that the treatment literally makes him into a pauper and so causes him to lose his princely status, but because he will believe the treatment is too low for him *given* that princely status. It is because he believes he is *not* lower in status that he regards the treatment as insulting. Similarly, a victim who is demeaned by an action believes he has experienced treatment which is insufficiently respectful of his value. Hence he finds the treatment insulting. The degree to which he is demeaned is the degree to which the treatment he experiences is too low for him.

Not to give people treatment appropriate to their value (i.e., not to give them the treatment they deserve) is to injure them. But this "objective" injury (an injury based upon what one takes the correct moral or societal facts about self-worth to be) is usually – although it need not be – associated with a subjective injury. If the person who has been wrongly treated *knows* this, then he will not only *be* but *feel* insulted. Moreover, he will probably feel pain from the insult, a pain with which we are all too familiar. *Why* "dishonoring" treatment can hurt us like this is something for which I do not have a reason-based explanation. Perhaps it is not the sort of thing which admits of a reason-based explanation.

The objective injury may not, to an observer's eye, correspond to a victim's subjective experience of injury. The latter can be seen to be too great or not great enough, and criticism of it presupposes that one believes the victim has accorded himself the wrong value. Thus, our view, or the victim's view, of when he is demeaned, depends upon the value which our, or his, "theory of human worth" accords him.

A theory of human worth tells one what sort of treatment is appropriate or required or prohibited for certain types of individuals on the basis of an assessment of *how valuable* these individuals are. Some philosophers follow Hobbes in thinking that any assessments of our value as individuals can only be instrumental: "The value, or worth, of a man is, as of all other things, his price; that is to say, so much as would be given for the use of his power."[11] Other philosophers insist that regardless of our price, the value which determines the kind of respect we should be accorded as persons is non-instrumental and objective. For example, according to Kant, by virtue of having the property of rationality, we are intrinsically valuable as ends-in-ourselves, so that we are all equal in worth and have the same rank relative to one another. Although I cannot go into this point here, perhaps the deepest quarrel the Kantian has with the utilitarian is that, because the utilitarian's theory incorporates people into the moral calculus solely as contributors to the common good (defined as the maximization of preference satisfaction, or happiness, or resources), they are treated only as instrumentally valuable.

But Kant has other opponents: There are objective theories of our intrinsic worth which do not accord all of us equal rank; consider, for example, views of human beings which propose that certain people, by virtue of being members of a race or caste or sex, are higher in value and deserving of better treatment than those who are of a different race or caste or sex. That women are more frequent targets than men for certain kinds of violence shows that many assailants see males, but not females, as having a value that rules out the infliction of this sort of violence. And those human beings (e.g., blacks in America) who have suffered unequal treatment, even slavery, know what it is like to be accorded value and rank considerably lower than those bestowed on other human beings (and which, in extreme cases, can be more like those accorded to animals).

One's theory of human worth may also be non-objective, denying that there are any properties by virtue of which we

---

11 Thomas Hobbes, *Leviathan*, ed. C. B. Macpherson (Harmondsworth: Penguin, 1965), Chapter 10, Paragraph 16.

have a certain instrinsic value and rank among our fellows. A theory of this sort may see any existing notions of relative standing based on assessments of "intrinsic worth" as, in reality, a societal invention, connected with or perhaps even the same as social standing in that culture. Alternatively, it might be perceived as a ranking that reflects subjective assessments of instrumental value; or as a ranking which varies from individual to individual depending upon what properties each uses to construct it and his judgement of the extent to which individuals manifest these properties.

Theories of human worth can also differ in the *way* in which worth is assigned. It can be assigned on the basis of certain criteria that are essentially non-competitive, as when a professor assigns grades to students by determining the "level" of their work according to certain criteria in such a way that it is possible in theory for every student to get an A. Or worth can be assigned using criteria that are inherently competitive, as when a professor compares her students and assigns a higher rank to those who do better in the comparison than to those who do worse. Similarly, theories of human worth may evaluate people to see whether they meet non-competitive criteria required for a certain value and rank (e.g., do they qualify as ends-in-themselves, as natural slaves?), or they may be assessed to see how far they are better or worse than one another, such that their particular positions can be determined on a scale ranking them in value. In what follows, when I speak of people losing 'value' or 'rank' I intend these phrases to be neutral between the two grading systems.

The evidence used to determine rank is also part of a theory of human worth. There are a variety of scales that measure us, such as tennis rankings, social rankings, intelligence rankings, rankings of work in a classroom. But such rankings need not be taken by us (or by others) to have anything to do with our worth as persons. For example, a prince might think he is equal in intrinsic worth to a pauper, but nonetheless insist that he receive treatment which recognizes his superior socio-political rank. On the other hand, a philosopher might

47

take strong exception to an action he interprets as slighting his considerable rank in the philosophical community, because that rank is taken by him to measure his worth as an individual. Scales which measure excellence as a parent or as an athlete or as an artist may or may not be regarded as relevant to the determination of our overall value as persons, that is, as an indication of the extent to which we are "important" or "impressive" as persons. What we take to be evidence of people's value is therefore part of a theory of what human value is.

Finally, whether or not we can gain or lose value (and thus rank) is part of this theory. Kant would insist that there is no way human beings can gain in value, and no way for them to lose their value unless their capacity to reason (and thus their very humanity) is badly damaged or destroyed. In contrast, Hobbes would insist that insofar as our value is instrumental, it is relatively easy for us to gain or lose worth, since these gains and losses depend on the skills, traits and abilities we gain or lose and on how the market prices these skills, traits and abilities.

Which theory of human worth is, properly speaking, a *moral* theory, is controversial. People in Western societies are apt to say that only some version of an egalitarian theory of human worth (e.g., that of Kant) can qualify as moral. But regardless of whether any hierarchical theory of worth merits the label "moral," it is still the sort of theory human beings tend to find enormously attractive and which, whether we like it or not, exerts political and social pressure even in societies whose official ideology is egalitarian. Indeed, we shall see in the next section that because certain forms of anger – which can be generated only if the agent holds a hierarchical (and indeed competitive) theory of human worth – are very common, it may be that many of us are only paying lip service to the egalitarian theories of worth which we tend to commend as appropriate foundations for our moral theorizing.

So, to summarize the preceding discussion: a theory of human worth involves, first, a conception of what it is for a human being to be valuable or of worth (e.g., is he of instru-

48

mental or of intrinsic value?); second, a conception of how, by virtue of their value, human beings should be ranked relative to one another (e.g., must they be ranked as equals, or should some be ranked higher than others?) in which an individual's rank determines her "standing" relative to other people; third, a conception of how evidence for that value is to be ascertained so that rank can be determined (e.g., competitively? non-competitively? with reference to what other measuring scales – job performance, athletic prowess, degree of virtue?); and fourth, a theory of how (if at all) human beings can gain or lose value (and thereby rank).

A person's view of her value and relative rank among her fellows determines whether she will interpret an action as demeaning. For example, she can feel demeaned by another's action if she believes she was the superior of this person but has received treatment that accorded her mere equality. A white person who is forced to sit next to a black person on a bus might believe this demeans her by making it appear that they are of equal rank and value and should thus be accorded equal treatment. Alternatively, one's theory can prevent one from feeling demeaned by treatment which seems, given *our* view of her value, demeaning. A rape counsellor once told me of a woman who failed to tell anyone that she had been raped by a man she knew because she thought this was the sort of thing women had to "take" from men.

The rape victim is actually an example of someone who has suffered a more severe kind of injury than simply being demeaned. Prior to the rape she received treatment persuading her that her value as a woman did not rule out this treatment by men. She is like a princess who believes, after receiving treatment appropriate only for a pauper, that she really is a pauper. Such a person cannot feel demeaned, because she has already suffered injury to her sense of self-worth. I will speak of this injury as the experience of *diminishment* following a wrongdoing. There are two ways in which one can feel, and believe oneself to be, diminished.

49

The first way involves a person taking the action as *evidence* that her value and rank are lower than she thought: this will lead her to worry that the wrongdoer's message may be right and that she has incorrectly accorded herself a value and rank, associated with a certain level of treatment, which she does not warrant. Note that she does not believe the action has effected a lowering of value and rank (so that, once again, it has not literally degraded her); instead she worries that it has *revealed* a rank that is lower than she thought. So what is lowered is her self-esteem.[12] Whereas someone who only experiences what she takes to be demeaning treatment will be quite sure that this treatment is too low for her, someone who feels diminished will receive treatment that raises in her mind the possibility that her estimate of her own value and rank may be incorrectly high. The higher the victim's degree of belief in this possibility, the more severe the injury to her self-esteem. If her faith in her own high worth is not completely undermined, she will still have some degree of belief that the wrongdoer's treatment of her was inappropriate given her high

---

12 In "How to Distinguish Self-Respect from Self-Esteem" (*Philosophy and Public Affairs* [Fall 1981], pp. 346–60), David Sachs distinguishes 'self-respect' from 'self-esteem.' The discussion here does not make use of that distinction; esteem and respect for oneself are taken to be the same thing. One might separate them, however, if one thought that a person could gain or lose self-esteem while maintaining the same respect for herself as a human being. Note that this way of talking presupposes a rather Kantian theory of human worth which makes someone's value objective, permanent and unchanging for as long as she remains a person, but which makes her achievements (e.g., on the job or in her avocation) or her moral performance that which determines her esteem for herself and which can change quite considerably over her lifetime. On this view, such measures of excellence are held to be irrelevant to the determination of one's worth as a person and it is that worth which is what one respects in oneself. To the extent that this sort of theory of human worth is adopted by a community, Sachs's distinction makes sense, but it need not be embraced. Hence in my discussion, I try to be as neutral as possible and so refrain from making a distinction that some theorists would find problematic: 'self-esteem' and 'self-respect' are thus treated as synonyms. Each refers to one's assessment of one's own value.

worth, and hence will believe (to that extent) that she has been demeaned. But to the extent that her sense of self-worth is shaken, any emotional protest against the insult will be mixed in her with the fear that the action wasn't an insult (or wasn't very much of an insult) after all.

The second way of feeling diminished involves taking the immoral action to have *done* something to *change* one's moral value, so that the action quite literally degrades one. For example, a victim can come to fear that he has lost value, and thus rank, if he interprets the assault as a "loss" to the wrongdoer which makes him "not as good as" she is in the way that a boxer's loss in the ring will result in his being ranked lower than the victor. Or he may fear that the action effects his degradation through the physical or psychological harms it has caused. There are certain ideals current in our society towards which we strive – for example, being the ideal athlete, the perfect mother, a "real" man. Actions can rob us of properties necessary to realize these ideals. A man paralyzed from the waist down by a gunshot wound can feel that the paralysis robs him of his manhood, or destroys his athletic dreams. A woman whose injuries mean that she can no longer bear children can feel that she has become a biological failure as a female. Feeling lowered in quality (i.e., losing ground relative to one's ideal) as a result of these injuries does not, in and of itself, mean feeling that one has suffered a loss of value as a human being. But such injuries can be linked by these victims (falsely, most of us think) to their worth as persons; they may worry or even believe that the injury from the action which makes them less than their ideal thereby makes them less valuable so that they no longer merit the same kind of respectful treatment they did before the injury. Once again, this form of diminishment comes in degrees. To the extent that the action has shaken one's confidence in one's value and rank, it has also diminished one. If it destroys all such confidence, the diminishment is complete.

This last form of diminishment, which is the experience of having been literally degraded, is the subjective experience of something one takes to be objectively possible. Depending upon what theory of human worth one accepts, one may not believe that such degradation can occur. So the objective injury (if it exists) may or may not go along with the subjective experience of such injury.

Is degradation or diminishment immoral? To answer this question, we need an analysis of what makes a human action not only a harm to a person but a *wrong*, and the preceding discussion provides us with one: [*A person wrongs another if and only if (while acting as a responsible agent) she treats him in a way that is objectively demeaning.*][13] On this definition those responsible agents whose treatment of others literally degrades or diminishes them (in either sense) commit wrongs, as opposed to mere harms, if (but only if) doing

13 This definition needs refinement in two ways. First, the notion of responsibility should be spelled out. I shall pass over this thorny problem here. Second, the definition needs to be expanded to ensure that it does not pick out as wrongs those harms which are mere accidents. A construction worker who is fully responsible for his actions does not commit a wrong when he accidentally hits another worker with a plank he is carrying (assuming he is exercising reasonable care). Such an action does not demean the one who is harmed. Should we therefore insert the notion of intentionality into the definition, so that it reads "if and only if . . . she *intentionally* treats him in a way that is objectively demeaning"? I think not. Doing so would make it difficult to capture the way in which *negligent* actions (which are never intentionally performed) are immoral. For example, if the construction worker ought to have been more careful while carrying the plank, and hit the other worker through carelessness, he is said to have acted immorally (i.e., in an objectively demeaning way) towards him, and yet he did not *intend* to hit him. So insisting on intentionality in order to distinguish wrongs from mere harms would result in turning negligent acts into the latter rather than the former, which seems incorrect. A wrong presupposes (as the lawyers say) a *mens rea* (i.e., guilty mind), but this notion has yet to receive precise formulation by anyone in the legal or philosophical communities. Nonetheless, such a formulation would have to be added to the definition of immoral actions to make it complete. Finally, note that this definition of immorality does not allow that a harm performed by someone judged not responsible is a wrong. Thus the harm committed by an insane person is a harm but not a wrong. This departs from Murphy's notion of what a wrong is. See Chapter 1, where he speaks of wrongs committed by insane people.

52

these things is itself objectively *demeaning,* that is, *disrespectful of these individuals' worth.* Such disrespect is therefore the foundation of any action's being wrong or immoral. We shall see later in this chapter and in Chapter 4 that not all diminishment qualifies as demeaning, and thus disrespectful, treatment. Indeed, I shall argue in Chapter 4 that a certain kind of diminishing treatment can even be morally required.

This definition of a wrong need not commit us to assuming that any responsible agent who commits a wrong is a wrongdoer. For example, a man who robs a bank because terrorists have threatened to kill his family unless he does so commits a wrong according to this definition, but we do not blame him for that wrong, and therefore do not consider him a wrongdoer. I shall not pursue an analysis of the distinction between 'performer of a wrong' and 'wrongdoer,' but the distinction itself will become important in the next section.

Note that I am explicitly linking assessments of worth to moral treatment. Since there are theories of human worth which are a far cry from what most of us take to be the foundations of moral behavior, this linkage may seem problematic. But as I noted earlier, the word 'moral' is really a success word used by us to commend the theory of worth that we believe to be right. Those who accept what we take to be objectionable theories do see them as moral, for example, South African whites who claim their evaluation of blacks as inferior is biblically based. For the purposes of this chapter, I will refrain from taking sides in the debate about which theory of human worth is "moral," that is, right (but in Chapter 4 I will show Kantian colors).

I will also have occasion later to comment on the fact that whereas suffering what one takes to be demeaning treatment is possible whether one's theory of human worth is egalitarian or not, experiencing diminishment in either of the two senses defined is possible only if one is drawn to (or accepts) a non-egalitarian theory of worth, one which grants that human beings can be very unequal in value and rank by virtue of some feature, action or ability.

III. RESENTMENT AND INDIGNATION

Resentment should not be confused with a kind of primitive defensive anger which any of us, as a species of animal, will feel towards our attackers. A dog will snarl and bite back if it is bitten by a snake, and similarly a human being will feel a kind of attacking rage – a kind of "bite back" response – towards one who has "bitten" her when he has mistreated her. But dogs are not usually understood to be resentful (or at least not resentful in the way we are). Resentment is (as Murphy appreciated) more than instinctive rage following an attack: it is an idea-ridden response.[14] What is its cognitive content?

The analysis in the preceding section showed that one can believe an action has demeaned one but still not suffer any injury to one's sense of self-worth in either of the senses defined, and that one can suffer such injury because of the action but not feel demeaned by it. However, it is perhaps most common to feel demeaned by the action but to *fear* that it has effected or revealed a low value and rank. This sort of mixed reaction to a wrong is central to the experience of resentment. People don't resent the injuries caused by earthquakes or tidal waves; they only resent injuries that have been deliberately inflicted by one who is able and required to respect – but does not – their value and rank. (So they may resent injuries produced by natural disasters if they believe God sent them.) Resentment is an emotion which reflects their judgement that the harmful treatment they experienced should not have been intentionally inflicted on them by their assailants insofar as it is *not* appropriate given their value and

14 The discussions of resentment, indignation and hatred in this chapter assume, as did Murphy's first chapter, a cognitivist theory of the emotions, one which makes some aspect of thought central to the definition of the emotion itself. As I interpret them, these emotions involve certain distinctive evaluative beliefs and desires which accompany any feelings or physiological changes in the person who experiences them. For discussion of this approach to emotions, see William Lyons, *Emotions* (Cambridge: Cambridge University Press, 1980).

rank. Hence it presupposes that they have experienced treatment they take to be demeaning, and therefore wrong. But not all demeaning treatments are resented; one resents only *culpable wrongdoings* – demeaning actions for which their agents can be not only held responsible but also *blamed*. (So we resent the bank robbery by a terrorist but not the bank robbery by a man who is told by the terrorist that his family will die unless he robs the bank.)[15]

Resentment is a kind of anger which protests the demeaning treatment to one who could and should have known better, and this protest is frequently linked with a verbal rebuke, reprimand or complaint directed at the insulter. To the extent that a person's resentment presupposes what we regard as the wrong theory of human worth, we will be critical of it (e.g., resentment arising from a racist appraisal of another's value). We will also criticize people for *not* feeling resentment (e.g., the rape victim in our previous example) if we believe this shows they have too low an evaluation of themselves. This example illustrates that the ability to feel resentment following a wrongdoing depends upon one's having enough sense of one's own worth to believe that the treatment is inappropriate and worthy of protest.

But resentment is more than just a protest. It is also an emotion which attempts a certain kind of *personal defense*. To see this, consider an insulting situation in a context in which there is *only* protest: imagine the response of a mother to her small child who has just wronged her by, let's say, lying to her. Of course it would be appropriate, even required, of the mother to protest the child's action by rebuking him, for example. But we would think it strange of the mother to *resent* the lie; surely, we would think, the mother is "above" resentment in such a situation. And if she did resent it, we might speak of her as feeling insecure.

15 Murphy links resentment to *responsible wrongdoings*. Since I build responsibility into the definition of wrong, I draw the distinction in terms of culpability. To put my point succinctly: we resent the wrongs committed by wrongdoers, but not the wrongs committed by (non-culpable) actors or the harms committed by non-responsible actors.

People such as this mother who are "beyond resentment" experience only the demeaning nature of the immoral action and thus the *insult* involved in the action, but do not, to any degree, experience diminishment (in particular, diminishment in the first sense defined earlier) because of the action. Of course they protest the action because they want to defend the value which makes the behavior wrong. And when they defend that value they are indirectly defending themselves. But self-defense is not the point of the protest. Their anger focuses on the fact that the wrongdoer has made a moral mistake; it does not focus on any fears they have about what the action has shown to be true about their value. Thus, unlike resentment, this anger is not intended as a *personal* anger, and the protest it involves is not intended as a *personal* defense.

I will use the word 'indignation' to denote this kind of anger, although that word is generally reserved for a very severe form of such anger which a non-resentful victim may not believe is necessary. Some readers may even think 'resentment' has a wide enough meaning to cover this impersonal form of protest, but because I want to distinguish the two forms, I will call the impersonal form 'indignation' and reserve 'resentment' for the personally defensive protest. Note that this analysis explains why indignation can be – and frequently is – experienced by someone who witnesses a wrong committed against someone other than herself, whereas resentment is normally an emotion experienced only by the one who has been harmed.[16]

What precisely does it mean to say that resentment is a personally defensive protest? I propose that resentment is not only a protest against the demeaning action but also *a defense against the action's attack on one's self-esteem.* Whereas indig-

---

16 This is not always true; for example, parents can resent harms done to their children, but this is the kind of exception that proves the rule. Resentment only seems possible for the parents because they regard their children as somehow an extension of themselves. Resentment of crimes against others is possible when, but only when, one connects oneself in a significant way to these others.

nant victims only experience being demeaned, resentful victims are both demeaned and *diminished in the first sense* by the action. As I said in the preceding section, someone can come to believe any of three things about an insulter's action: (1) that the insulter has made a mistake about his value and rank and is treating him in a way that is too low given his value and rank; *or* (2) that the insulter is right to think his status is lower so that the treatment is permissible; *or* (3) that the insulter is right to think that his worth can be lowered and that it is permissible for him to do so. Those who cannot resent such harmful treatment accept that either (2) or (3) is true. Those who are "beyond resentment" are certain that (1) is true and that (2) and (3) are false. But those who *do* resent the harmful treatment have some degree or belief in (1) and *want* to believe (1) while nonetheless *fearing* that (2) or (3) may be true. The treatment has raised a doubt about their value and rank.

To be precise, resentment consists not only of a characteristic "feeling" frequently associated with certain physiological changes in one's body (e.g., an accelerated heartbeat) but also of the following:

1. A *fear* that the insulter has acted permissibly in according you treatment that would be appropriate only for one who is low in rank and value. Your fear can be analyzed as involving:
   a. *some degree of belief* that the insulter is right to treat you as low in rank and value (i.e., you neither fully believe it nor fully disbelieve it);
   b. a *wish* that the belief described in item 1a is not true, so that you are not low in rank and value (i.e., you wish to have no degree of belief that you are as low in rank and value as his action assumes you to be).
2. An *Act of Defiance:* you "would have it" that the belief in item 1a is false (i.e., you would have it that you are high in rank and value).

This act of defiance is the heart of the emotion. The resenter *denies* to himself (and anyone else) that he is low in rank and value, and thereby defies the appearance (implicit

57

in the demeaning action) that he is. This defiance is engendered by his wish that his value and rank are high. It is the person's battle against accepting the lower standing.[17] Of all the concepts in this chapter which need further philosophical explanation, this concept of defiance is at the top of the list. In what follows, although I do not analyze it, I shall try at least to describe it as I investigate the emotions in which it figures.

How much sympathy we have for this person's battle depends upon the theory of human worth which determines the rank he is defending. We applaud the rape victim who fights the message (which she half believes) that she lacks value relative to her attacker. We are disgusted by the white woman's defiance of the black man's claim that she is no better than he. Nonetheless, no matter how much we applaud resenters, there is something worrying about their defensive response. How can one succeed in defying the truth of something that one half believes? Resenters are vulnerable, and as we will explore later, their defiant act requires buttressing if they are going to be able to gain a high degree of belief in what they wish to believe.

Let us now consider, more precisely, how resentment is different from indignation. Consider those people who are "beyond resentment" in the sense that their belief in their standing is so strong that demeaning actions cannot call it into question. For example, although it meant his torture and death, Jesus is not presented in the Gospels as someone who feared that the betrayal, the torture or the crucifixion either effected or revealed a loss of moral value or rank. Indeed, while on the cross Jesus pitied and expressed concern for those who brought about his crucifixion. This is a very remarkable reaction to a wrongdoing; it is the experience of the harm involved in the wrongdoing, as well as the experience of the demeaning treatment (and any pain that experi-

---

17 Note that this analysis treats resentment as an emotion which furthers certain purposes we all have. See the general discussion of this point in note 22 of this chapter.

ence might generate within him), but without any damage to self-esteem which such severe wrongdoings ordinarily inflict.[18] People such as this, who regard their assailants as merely pitiful, already have a high degree of belief in what the resentful victim is struggling to have full confidence in, namely, that the wrongdoer's action has failed to respect their true value. So the indignant person experiences neither the fear nor the defiance which is characteristic of resentment.

Nonetheless, indignation contains a *kind* of fear and defiance. Indignant people fear that not to oppose a wrongdoer's challenge to someone's value may be to encourage future challenges to people's value. Hence they defy these defiers of value. They don't fight to believe in something they (only) wish to believe in; they fight for something they *do* believe in and attack the opponent of it so that she won't undermine its power in the community. Henceforth I shall refer to the view of others' value conveyed by the wrongdoer's action and the target of their opposition as the wrongdoer's 'immoral cause.' Indignant people see their moral cause as competing with the wrongdoer's immoral cause, and they aim to defeat it.

So, to be precise, *indignation is the emotional protest against immoral treatment whose object is the defense of the value which this action violated,* whereas *resentment is an emotion whose* object

18 But it may nonetheless have been a painful experience. Indignant people may differ to the degree that they experience pain as a result of the action they take to be demeaning. The mother in our example is unlikely to feel any personal *hurt* or psychological "bite" from the child's lie. Somehow the child is not the kind of person who can inflict that bite (perhaps because the mother does not think the child's view of her own lack of value has any credibility), although he can fail to respect her value, and so in an objective sense demean her. But as I pointed out in the preceding section, people who demean us are generally able to make us feel bad. Even if they don't in any way do something to make us doubt our self-worth, so that there is no fear in our response to them and we are completely confident that they have treated us wrongly, they can still *wound* us by their treatment. I cannot help but think that even if Jesus didn't resent Peter's denials, he was still deeply hurt by them.

is the defiant reaffirmation of one's rank and value in the face of treatment calling them into question in one's own mind.

There is nothing pleasant about the feeling of indignation. However, the feeling of resentment has a certain pleasure to it. I suspect that we enjoy it not only because we enjoy asserting what we wish our own worth to be, but also because the emotion encourages the belief that the wrongdoer is "morally worse" than his victim insofar as he bears the stain of sin, of which the victim is free. The emotional protest against one's victimization can be a way to assert that one really is *better* than one's wrongdoer, not in the sense that one is morally more valuable than he is, but in the sense that he merits moral disapproval in a way his victim does not. (A Kantian would say that both are ends-in-themselves, but the wrongdoer has shown himself to have a will which is, at least on this occasion, bad, whereas the victim has not.) In the attempt to repair a battered sense of self-worth, this thought can be both useful and welcome. It is also perilously close to the beliefs that are constitutive of hatred.

IV. RESENTMENT AND HATRED

Hatred is frequently confused with resentment. But whereas the object of hatred can be and frequently is a person, the object of resentment is an *action*. When resentment is directed at a person, it is in response to what he did, not who or what he is. Hence we say "I hate you," and "I resent what you *did*" but not "I resent *you*" (unless 'resent' is used to mean 'envy').

This semantic difference directs us to the substantive difference between resentment and hatred. But to pursue this difference we first need to see how the word 'hatred' covers a *family* of negative emotional responses. For example, I can hate a person in the way that I hate cloudy weather or snowmobiling or mosquitoes. "I can't stand that man," I may tell my friend at a party. "He talks my ear off every time I meet him." This is what I will call *simple hatred:* It is an intense dislike for or a strong aversion to an object perceived as profoundly unpleasant, accompanied by the wish to see the odious thing removed or eliminated. This sort of hatred is the opposite of "simple love," the attraction one feels towards objects one finds greatly pleasurable, from sunny weather and chocolate to charming people at parties.

Much less simple is the kind of hatred towards human beings which is experienced in many moral contexts; for example, I may speak of hating the Nazis for what they did to the Jews, or hating the South African whites for their violence against blacks. I will call this *moral hatred*: it is an aversion to someone who has identified himself with an immoral cause or practice, prompted by moral indignation and accompanied by the wish to triumph over him and his cause or practice in the name of some fundamental moral principle or objective, mostly notably justice. Initially it seems as if this kind of hatred is surprisingly impersonal: one is not really attacking the person so much as the immoral principles with which he has identified himself. But, as we shall discuss later, these principles can get tangled up with his character and beliefs in the same way a cancer can get mixed up with the healthy cells of one's body, so that hating them can come to mean hating him. Moral hatred is the opposite of what one might call *moral love*, that is, the attraction one feels towards someone whom one believes has identified himself with a moral cause or objective, combined with the desire to see him and his moral cause prevail – the kind of emotion felt towards people like Martin Luther King, Jr., or Gandhi.

I shall discuss moral hatred at some length later. For now I want to distinguish both of these forms of aversion from the sort of hatred one tends to feel towards those who have personally brought harm to one (where that harm may or may not be a moral wrong) – the sort of hatred one feels when one experiences *spite* or *malice* or when one "nurses a grudge" against a wrongdoer. Note that one can only feel this form of hatred towards a *person*; it makes no sense to feel spite towards a crime. So this kind of hatred can only be a personal animosity, and as I shall now argue, this is because the person's action generates a *competitive response* to *that person*.[19]

I shall argue that this sort of hatred can be (but need not be) precipitated by resentment. In the preceding section I analyzed resentment as an emotion which contained fear that one had been made or revealed to be lower in rank and value than one previously had thought one was, combined with a defiant denial of the fall. Clearly, a resenter is in an unstable situation – she is trying to defy what she half believes. How does she keep from succumbing to what may be the unpleasant reality? Hatred is not only an emotion with a characteristic feeling and certain accompanying physiological changes; it is also a strategy for getting support for the hater's wish that she was not diminished by the wrongdoing, and this introduction to it should already suggest my conclusion that it is an irrational strategy for restoring self-esteem. But I am getting ahead. To understand hatred, we need answers to two questions: How is malicious or spiteful hatred a "strategy"? And exactly how does it fail to achieve the hater's objective?

To understand its strategic character, first consider nonhateful strategies resenters might use to buttress their defiance of the wrongdoer's message. The rational way of doing so would be to go out and secure evidence showing that the feared belief is false. The problem with this strategy, however, is that, even assuming one had a clear sense of where to find such evidence, the evidence once found may point to the belief's being true. Hence our vulnerable resenter would prefer a strategy that will *ensure* that she finds support only for the belief's falsity.

So she might try employing what I will call the 'unscrupulous recognition strategy.' Those who try it aim to support their wished-for rank and value by dishonestly securing *other* people's opinion that what they wish for is correct, presumably because they take other people's opinions to be signifi-

---

19 I am greatly indebted to Philippa Foot, who directed me to the competitive element in hatred and who thereby sparked this line of analysis.

cant or even decisive evidence of their worth. Now an honest recognition-seeker would lay out for those whose opinions she sought the reasons why she feared (in light of the insulter's action) that her rank and value were lower than she thought, and then ask them to judge her true rank and value in the light of the evidence, admitting that her own judgement on this matter is not to be trusted. ("Do you really think," a rape victim might ask a friend, "that women have to take this kind of thing from men?") The problem with this strategy is that the resenter may learn from others that they believe she really *isn't* as high in rank and value as she would like. For many resenters, this is exactly the last thing they want to hear. So they try to gain from others their wished-for value and rank by rigging in some way the evidence put to others in their favor. For example, they might be careful to conceal from them what they take to be the evidence of their lower rank and value (e.g., evidence which the insulting action taken against them might provide). Indeed, conceal-ment of the evidence isn't even necessary if they can get the recognition they want from people who have as much reason to ignore the counter-evidence as they do, such as friends or relatives or people who want similar evidence about them-selves ignored. Or they might misdescribe the episode that could be taken to show they have a lower value and rank, so that, as *they* tell it, the episode does not suggest their dimin-ishment.

But unscrupulous recognition-seekers are engaging in a self-defeating strategy; that is, their method of achieving a secure sense of their high worth will actually prevent them from achieving that goal. Suppose they succeed in gaining from others the recognition they wish; then they will find it impossible to believe it, precisely because they know it has been granted by these others without taking account of the evidence against it. They will feel like frauds, imposters, emperors without clothes. No matter how high the others elevate them through their recognition, that recognition can-not comfort them, because they cannot believe it has been correctly given. So this strategy fails because it is self-defeating: obtaining the desired objective – getting evidence of one's high standing through the recognition of others – involves not allowing them to take account of the evidence against it; but after "rigging" the outcome of their judgement in this way, one cannot take their recognition as evidence for the desired standing.

There are other kinds of self-defeating, and hence irrational, recognition strategies. One of them is discussed in the Master-Slave Dialectic by Hegel in his *Phenomenology:*[20] it involves seeking recognition of superiority from someone whom one wishes to believe inferior; I will call it the 'superstar' recognition strategy. Let me illustrate, using the following story: I was recently told of a philosopher whose work was impressive, who enjoyed a high reputation, and who wanted very much to believe that he was one of the finest philosophers in the country (if not *the* finest), but who continually worried that he was not. Thus, when he attended conventions he would seek out people who would discuss his work and praise it, and beam with satisfaction as the praise was given. But those who knew him knew that the satisfaction was momentary, and that his fears would quickly return. The person who related this story to me puzzled over the quick return of these fears, but it is not, I think, hard to see why this philosopher was constantly plagued by them, given the way in which he tried to shore up his shaky sense of self-worth. He could only believe that he was a superior philosopher (= superior person) if that judgement came from someone whose philosophical acuity and originality were at least as great as his own, but since he was determined to believe that he was better than those who complimented him, he could not trust their evaluation of his work and abilities. So the method he chose to buttress his wished-for sense of self-worth continually defeated that very goal.

Consider a mirror image of the superstar recognition strat-

---

20 In his Master-Slave Dialectic in the *Phenomenology of Spirit* (see the translation by A. V. Miller [Oxford: Oxford University Press, 1977], pp. 111–19), Hegel tends to confuse the recognition and hatred strategies in his talk of mastery. In this chapter, I try to differentiate them.

egy. I'll call it the 'neophyte' recognition strategy. To picture it, imagine a new member of the faculty at a law school, who wants to believe that her abilities as a lawyer and legal theorist are considerable, but who lacks full confidence in her abilities among faculty far older and more prominent. So she goes to those whom she sees as more distinguished than she in order to get recognition from them that her work and abilities are as good as or better than theirs. But she is no more reassured than our superstar. If she trusts their judgement, this is because she sees them as better than she, in which case their approval can only mean that she *isn't* as good as they are. And if she doesn't trust it on the grounds that she wants to believe herself better, then she is in the same position as the superstar, unable to use recognition by others to establish her superiority insofar as the others' judgement is demeaned.

I will argue that hatred, in the form of either malice or spite, is yet another of these self-defeating strategies for shoring up a shaky sense of one's own worth. Because malice and spite are, on my analysis, slightly different strategies for doing this, let me discuss them separately.

First consider malice. Imagine someone who has deliberately injured you badly – suppose he has physically assaulted you. If you maliciously hate him, you see him as "low" and "base." Your hatred may prompt you to try to "get him," or "hurt him back," or "get even." You vilify him either behind his back or to his face. You may seek his public censure and take pleasure in the thought of his public humiliation. Whereas you seek to see a beloved one increase, you desire to see this hated person decrease, either by losing self-esteem or by literally losing value. But what good does his diminishment (in either sense) bring you?

Perhaps you value that diminishment for its own sake, so that your hate is a display of what one might call "negative other-interestedness."[21] But this does not seem right; there

---

21 Robert Adams proposed this idea to me. My rejection of the idea that hatred is a display of negative other-interestedness plants me squarely

is far too much human enthusiasm for this emotion (especially among the most selfish of us) to make it plausible that the only self-regarding benefit to be gained from it is an unintended side effect of the pursuit of a disinterested objective. But to find the self-regarding good which malicious haters pursue, we must figure out how diminishment of another can be a good for them. Only then will we discover the *point* of malice.[22]

Consider that one situation in which you are benefited by harm to another is when you are in competition with him. In a race you are benefited by your opponents' exhaustion when it allows you to win. An orange grower in Florida benefits from frost damage to crops in California if it allows him to sell his product at a higher price in a competitive market. So we have an explanation for a hater's pleasure at the thought of her opponent's demise if we see her as competing to win against this person.

For what is she competing? Consider again the two ways in which a wrongdoer's immoral action can damage the victim's self-esteem. She may worry that his victory reveals that she has less value and rank than she thought she had, or she

on the side of Kant, who maintains both in *Lectures on Ethics* (trans. Louis Infield [Indianapolis: Hackett, 1930]) and in *Religion Within the Limits of Reason Alone* (trans. Theodore M. Greene and Hoyt H. Hudson [New York: Harper and Row, 1960]) that human beings do not desire harm for its own sake (a motivation Kant calls "devilish") but, rather, desire harm to derive some benefit to themselves. Note that the following discussion of malicious hatred bears striking similarity to Kant's analysis of "grudge" in *Lectures on Ethics* (pp. 215–23).

22 While rejecting the Sartrean idea that emotions are had for a purpose, Lyons (*Emotion*, pp. 186–8) does endorse the idea that some emotions are useful to (or serve the purpose of) the person who has them. Nonetheless, he argues that this is not true of hatred, which he believes is not in any way useful or conducive to our basic interests. My analysis aims to show that while this may be true, those who hate do not *believe* it is true. I argue that hatred is regarded as personally useful insofar as it furthers a basic interest in the advancement of our own worth (what Hobbes would call the desire for glory). And the very fact that hatred is something we tend to enjoy, even relish on occasion (however much we may be ashamed of our enjoyment), is psychological evidence that we take the emotion to be useful to us.

may worry that his action has effected a lowering of her value and rank (and fear that it may even have been permissible for him to do this to her). Now a resenter who wishes to restore her self-esteem may not think the wrongdoer elevated himself by causing her to feel diminished in either or both of these ways; she may only fear or believe that she has fallen relative not only to him but to others as well. As long as she believes this, diminishing her opponent in return does not make sense; this resenter wants to raise herself up, and she does nothing to achieve this objective if she works to bring him low. But a resenter will pursue her own elevation by attacking the value and rank of her opponent if she interprets his diminishment of her in a competitive way, and when she does so she bears malice towards her opponent. A malicious hater sees the assailant's action against her as representing a loss in a competition *for rank* with him. Her own fall was the means by which another elevated himself relative to her and to others. For example, she may believe that her opponent's action represents a competitive victory over her which allows him to move up the ladder and forces her to move down. Or she may see the wrongdoer's action against her as potentially signifying qualities that place him higher and her lower on the ranking ladder than she had thought previously. Compare the way in which tennis rankings work: a lower-ranked player who beats a higher-ranked player moves up in rank and causes the higher-ranked player to drop in standing because his victory signifies superior tennis abilities; similarly, a hater may fear that the hated one has beaten her in a way that shows that he meets the criteria for a higher standing, and she meets the criteria for a lower standing.

Malicious haters respond to this competitive threat in a competitive way. Like the resenter, these haters defy their feared loss of value and rank. They do so in one of two ways. Either this sort of hater "would have it" that the ranking of the two of them which was revealed or created by the hated one's triumph over him is not correct, or else, even if it is correct, he "would have it" that it is not permanent. A malicious hater goes on to support what he wishes to believe either by reinterpreting the world so that his opponent is diminished or by taking action designed to reveal or effect the other's diminishment. And diminishment (in either sense) of the opponent is valued as a means to the hater's ultimate objective, namely, showing or effecting for himself a high rank (at the very least, a higher rank than it appears he has, given what he has suffered).

What do I mean when I say malicious hatred may involve a defiant reinterpretation of the world? Consider someone who inwardly seethes at an enemy whom she fears has "won" over her in some way. What happens when she inwardly seethes? Using words that vilify her enemy and elevate herself, she projects onto the world the rankings she would have them occupy. She "sees" him as low, and herself as high. And like an unscrupulous scientist casting around for evidence to support her theory, the hater uses anything which might count as evidence for what she wishes to be their relative value and rank to support her defiant view of their real standings. For example, she might make use of things she has heard people say about him, or psychological theories which call his achievements into question, or prominent character defects – anything which could serve as grist to her mill by indicating he is really lower than he appears on the ranking ladder. She may also imagine herself winning various hypothetical contests with him, thereby lowering him and raising herself in her own mind. Her dim view of him may even arouse emotions of disgust and outrage at his action and character. And through it all, she takes pleasure in the thought of his diminishment because she believes it represents a relative gain for her on the ranking ladder.

But such private reinterpretations, if the malicious hater tries them, are rarely enough for her. The relative valuations she projects onto the world have their source in a wish. And she cannot simply claim that she believes these valuations; the fear driving the defiance tends to undermine her belief in them, and her unscrupulous use of evidence does little to confirm them effectively in her own mind. Hence, malicious haters will frequently try to find *new* evidence for the valuations they wish to be true.

To this purpose, a malicious hater may try something like the unscrupulous recognition strategy, hoping that others' good opinion will help her to believe that the theory she desires to believe is true, but as we discussed, this strategy is self-defeating. So she may vilify the opponent to his face, trying to extract from him a confession of his inferiority, which would be another kind of evidence that the relative valuations she wishes for are true. (And do we hesitate to repent of our crimes precisely because we fear it will be interpreted by our victims as a kind of victory over us which lowers us, or which is, in and of itself, an admission of our inferiority?)

More commonly, a malicious hater engages in what are called "vengeful" actions which involve controlling or harming or mastering her enemy. By winning against him in this way, she hopes to diminish him, either by revealing or by making him to be lower, and such diminishment is perceived as an indirect way of elevating herself.

The action threatening the malicious hater's sense of self-worth and relative standing need not be what we would normally consider immoral. For example, in 1 Samuels, Chapters 17–18, King Saul is described as hating David (and seeking to have him killed) because of David's prowess as a warrior. In Saul's eyes such excellence was evidence that David was a superior leader. David thus became a hated rival for the highest rank in the community, and the object of Saul's murderous intentions. Note, however, that although David's action was not immoral and was not even directed at Saul, it still threatened Saul's social and political rank in the community, which he understood to determine his value as a person, and hence was an action whose message he felt called upon to defy.

Nor is it necessary that the malicious hater, in order to be threatened, fear that her assailant's action has shown her to be inferior to him; she need only fear that it has either changed or forced a reevaluation of their relative rankings, lowering her and raising him. To give an example, I once knew a teenage boy who was in the track club at school, and who decided that he wanted to race a female friend of his. They staged the race and, to his dismay, she won. He was mortified because he had lost to a girl, and angry with *her* for what he thought she had done to him, but her victory did not suggest to him that she was of higher standing than he. Instead it suggested that relative to other males he was of rather low rank because a female could beat him in a race. He responded to her hatefully, verbally abusing her in person and maligning her behind her back. The boy perceived her action as raising her rank as a female while lowering his (still higher) rank as a male; he believed that regaining the rank her victory had taken from him required that he master her on other playing fields.

One may even maliciously hate a person one believes has a higher ranking than oneself if one takes exception to action which suggests that one is *more* inferior than one thought. A peasant's hatred of the lord whose onerous taxes are hurting him may never dream of showing he is the lord's superior, but may long to attack the lord and achieve victory over him in order to upgrade himself relative to the lord.

We call these malicious haters "vindictive" because they are trying to vindicate a controversial faith in their own relative rank and value. Because they are after this kind of vindication, malicious haters always welcome those actions of others which might manifest the opponent's lowliness, and which therefore might be taken indirectly to suggest that they are elevated in rank and value. But I suspect we tend to think that vindication is surest when we win a direct competition with the ones we hate. Their defeat at our hands provides the best evidence for our claims not only that they are lower but also that we are higher.

We now have an explanation for the semantic difference between the words 'hatred' (understood to denote malicious hatred) and 'resentment.' Resentment is an emotional response to an action in which one defies what one experiences as the diminishing message in the action. The resenter directs an attack at the one who diminished her, but she is actually attacking what he, through his action, said about her; she does not attack *him*. The malicious hater, however, does mount an attack on the one who performed the diminishing action, because she sees it as a way to defy his diminishing message. This kind of hatred may therefore serve the objectives of resentment insofar as it generates action designed to give evidence that one is in fact higher in value and rank than the wrongdoer's action presumed. However, this hatred may be experienced apart from any feelings of resentment. For example, if Saul is convinced that David's success as a warrior has elevated David over himself, he would not resent what David had done (because he would not read David's action as in any way demeaning him), but he would nonetheless maliciously hate David because of the elevation effected by David's victories, where that hate would involve the defiant belief that Saul will be able to degrade David and thereby prove himself David's superior. So even in situations where no demeaning action (i.e., no immoral action) has occurred, malicious hatred is possible if there has been action that is believed to have diminished one; the malice may arise if one is intent on proving or making oneself upgraded relative to the diminisher.

What is perhaps most fascinating about this sort of hatred from a philosophical standpoint is that, as with resentment, one can only experience it if one believes or fears that human beings can differ in rank. Indeed, malice presupposes not only that one believes oneself to be ranked on a ladder that has more than one rung, but also that one is in competition with others for the higher rungs. Underlying this emotion, therefore, is a non-egalitarian, competitive grading system, and thus an anti-Kantian theory of worth (and how many philosophers who profess the Kantian theory are nonetheless prone to feel malice, showing that they are susceptible to the theory of unequal worth the emotion presupposes?). It is not hard, I think, to understand why people tend to reject the Kantian view; the problem with a view that accords us equal worth is that no one can be better, or more valuable, on that view, than any other person. And many of us long for supe-

71

riority. Value-egalitarianism is especially unpopular among those whose physical or intellectual skills might be thought to provide grounds for a higher value. But if one takes seriously the idea that some people might be worth more than others, one lays oneself open to fears that one's worth might be lower than that of others, fears which can lead to an emotion which involves a desire for one's own elevation through another's degradation.[23]

The benefits of malicious hatred, however, are illusory[24] because, like the irrational recognition strategies we discussed, malice is self-defeating (an idea also proposed by Jon Elster).[25] Consider a normal and healthy competitive situation. A low-seeded tennis player desires to improve her ranking, so she plays a high-seeded player and wins. She is elated, and believes that her ranking has been raised because she has triumphed over one who is recognized, by both herself and others, to be of very high rank. In general, she finds that the higher the respect she and others pay to her opponents, the sweeter the victory is for her – because the more the victory exalts her. This is reflected in how the victory determines their relative rankings: If the victory elevates the

23 This form of hatred is first cousin to another vice: envy. But envy is a bit more honest than malice or spite. A person who envies someone does not fear but actually believes in that person's higher rank relative to her. There is no attempt to defy the reality of her position, but there is certainly a wish that the envied person fall in rank, where (as in spite or malice) that fall is thought to raise the envier's rank.

24 Kant would probably try to make this point by insisting that there is no way an attack on another person can possibly show him to be lower in moral status, because people are equal in worth and thus in standing, and their worth cannot be damaged as long as they retain their rationality. But victims of wrongdoings frequently don't believe this; if they are to be persuaded not to hate their wrongdoers, they must be persuaded that the good which hatred promises is just an illusion. The argument I construct attempts to show this.

25 I am greatly indebted to Jon Elster for noting the relevance of the Master-Slave Dialectic to the experience of hatred in his *Ulysses and the Sirens* (Cambridge: Cambridge University Press, 1979), pp. 161–5. Note, however, that the argument I present is not explicitly Hegel's, which is really an argument against what I have already discussed as the 'superstar' recognition strategy.

winning player substantially, this is because the losing player is and continues to be highly respected, so that her loss is not understood to produce a substantial fall in rank. And if the loss *is* understood to show that the losing player is very low in rank, the victorious player receives little elevation in rank from the victory. Thus *in a normal competitive situation, there is nothing self-defeating about seeking to win against an opponent to elevate oneself.*

In contrast, hatred prompts an abnormal, *twisted* and ultimately self-defeating competition. If our tennis player hates the top-seeded player, then she hopes, by winning over her, to show her to be *bad* – to degrade her substantially, and such diminishment is supposed to be a way of restoring or proving her own status. Yet should she succeed (in her own mind or in others' minds) in making this point, her opponent's degradation causes the victory to lose its elevating power. Suppose people respond to the bad tennis player's victory by saying, "My! You beat Martina Navratilova! She has really lost her tennis ability!" To the extent that her victory succeeds in persuading people that Martina is bad, then her victory over Martina is unimpressive and she doesn't get the elevation she craved. It is only by winning against someone who was and continues to remain *good* that she is elevated in rank. Thus the hateful player who insists that the person over whom she triumphs is no good shows only that she can win against bad players, which gives her no real exaltation. As John Donne (whom Jon Elster quotes when discussing hatred)[26] puts it, "Lest my being nothing lessen thee, / If thou hate me, take heed of hating me."

The futility of this sort of hatred is also a popular theme of old Western movies. An avenger uses the threat of death to master a hated wrongdoer in order to diminish him. Frequently this involves "making him crawl" before the avenger. And any show of remorse by the now terrified and lowly wrongdoer is perceived as proof of the elevated status of the avenger. But as he looks upon the wretched and

---

26 From "The Prohibition," quoted by Elster, p. 161.

pathetic figure of the wrongdoer, the avenger invariably finds that he is getting no pleasure from his victory. He has shown that the wrongdoer is nothing, so that now he is the lord of nothing. Finally aware that the whole strategy has been unsuccessful, the avenger bitterly drops his gun.

In the examples considered thus far, the malicious hater wants to win a competition in order to *reveal* the other's lower status; but is malice more successful when it motivates an attempt to *effect* lower status? No; for suppose the hater succeeds in changing the one whom she hates so that now he is inferior. Damaging someone (e.g., paralyzing him, killing him) in order to gain superiority over him is rather like trying to become the most beautiful person in the kingdom by killing or disfiguring anyone who might be more beautiful. Doing this doesn't change the fact that they *were* prettier (or superior in value) before the disfigurement. The hater changes the individual she hates in order to diminish her; yet by doing so she does not and cannot change the fact that the hated one really was better than she before the change.

Still, doesn't the hater achieve some consolation by effecting the change, and attaining superiority now? No; for she has made herself the superior of one who has been rendered low in rank, and what glory is there in this? Killing or disfiguring prettier people only makes one more beautiful than a corpse or a person with a scarred face, and how great a sign of one's beauty is this? The hater wants to be more beautiful than other beautiful people. And similarly, the hater wants to achieve elevation over a living and healthy individual rather than over a mere corpse or psychologically mutilated remnant of a person. Yet, by damaging a person in order to make him inferior, the hater makes the elevation impossible. There is a children's story that makes this point nicely: In order to capture a kingdom, an evil wizard concocts a gaseous substance that spreads through the air and turns all the people in the kingdom into sheep. He easily becomes their leader, but finds no exaltation in this. What glory is there in being first among sheep?

So malicious hatred is self-defeating. If you hate in this

way, then in support of your defiant claim to be elevated relative to your enemy, you project onto the world (and possibly take action to effect) his diminishment relative to you. But the more you succeed in that diminishment (either by effecting it or by revealing it), the less successful you are at showing yourself to have a high rank. The more exalted you feel by any victories over him, the higher the rank you are in fact according him, and the more you have failed either to effect his diminishment or to reveal him as low in rank.

So why did hatred seem like such a good idea in the first place? I must now explain the illusion that malicious hatred is a good response to an insult. To this end, consider that there is *no point* in pursuing elevation relative to someone you already believe to be diminished relative to you. But if you hate, you *don't* believe in your opponent's diminishment; in fact you *fear* (have some degree of belief in, but wish not to be true) his elevation relative to you. It is the half-belief in his elevation that makes the thought of your victory over him so sweet – any victory is sweet when it is over a high-ranking opponent, because it is a victory which genuinely elevates you. But your hatred involves the defiant denial of the truth of this half-belief; you are intent on showing that he isn't elevated, and the sweetness of your victory over him – which is tied to the relative elevation the victory effects for you – diminishes to the extent that you succeed in showing him to be bad.

To put the self-defeating character of malice as succinctly as possible: the malicious hater's wish for a high rank and value is combined with a strategy for attaining it which assumes his belief in his own low rank and value; if the hater succeeds in his strategy, the rank and value for which he longs elude him. So whether or not malice is immoral, this argument establishes that it is *stupid,* as the common saying, "Stop hating: you're paying him too much of a compliment" tries to convey.[27]

---

27 Note that if you have previously felt malice towards others, this may adversely affect your ability to buttress your own sense of self-worth,

Let us now turn to spite, which is a close cousin to malice. Whereas a malicious hater wants to achieve mastery over the hated one in order to be elevated above (or relative to) him, the spiteful hater wants "company" at the bottom, and so desires to bring the hated one down to her level. The following archetypal case of spite was described to me by someone who found it recounted in a "Dear Abby" column: A man wrote to Abby to tell her about a woman he had met at a party. They got on well, he took her back to his apartment, and they made love. The next morning he awoke and found her gone, but the following message was written in lipstick on the bathroom mirror: "Welcome to the Wonderful World of AIDS." Within a year the man was diagnosed as carrying the AIDS antibody. He wrote Abby wanting to know why this woman had done such a thing to him, when he had never in any way hurt her.[28]

To answer the question is to uncover how the spite felt by the AIDS victim was a strategy to achieve some purpose she had. The following analysis of her strategy is proposed as an answer to the question: Here is a woman who is surely mortified at what the AIDS virus has done to her worth. Not only has it made her terminally ill, but it has also given her what some people consider a dirty person's disease, or even a punishment from God. Hence she feels very low in value relative to her fellow human beings, and angry at most of them for

because the standards and criteria you previously used to diminish them may recoil onto you. If they are judged low by such standards, it may also be that *you* are low by the same standards. Your fear that this is so can become part of the evidence that must be concealed in your pursuit of others' recognition (unless you can find people who judge by, and also fear the personal implications of, these same standards, in which case they have as much reason to ignore this evidence against you as you do). The danger of the recoil of your judgements, especially in the context of hatred, is surely behind Jesus' injunction "Pass no judgement, and you will not be judged. For as you judge others, so you will yourself be judged, and whatever measure you deal out to others will be dealt back to you" (Matt. 7:1–3). We shall discuss this injunction further in Chapter 4.

28 Alas, the reference is lost. The story appeared in her column in the fall of 1987.

occupying a position that is so much higher than her own. So why not do what she can to bring them down to her level? To the extent that she succeeds, she'll have company at the bottom. But what good is such company? Why is Misery supposed to like it?

I propose that a spiteful person wants the company because, even if she can't do anything to elevate herself, she can nonetheless succeed, by diminishing others to her level or below, in "changing the value curve" on which everyone is ranked, so that she will look better relative to others than she now does. Of course our AIDS victim has little hope (thank God!) of infecting enough people to make any substantial difference in (what she takes to be) that curve in our society, but other spiteful people might be in situations in which they are much more effective in carrying out their curve-changing strategy. Imagine a child who, unable to have the same expensive doll as her friend, breaks the friend's doll; or a man who, after being denied a promotion ensures that his rival cannot get the promotion either. Such people do something to try to take away what they believe is the advantage held by those who, in their view, are ranked higher than they are, and in this way they hope to achieve equality. And such equality, I am arguing, is a *good* for them, and thus desired, because they see it as an indirect way of elevating themselves. The B student who makes sure the A students can't effectively study for the exam can succeed in changing the curve so that he gets an A; similarly, the spiteful hater who takes away the hated one's advantage and thereby brings him down to her level believes that by doing so she can indirectly improve her own ranking.

But whether or not the spiteful hater's strategy is effective in changing the curve, it will always be self-defeating as a way of achieving elevation. Consider that the AIDS victim's best way of changing the value curve among human beings is to destroy all but herself: then she can truly be the finest human being on earth. Such "stature" is, of course, ridiculous. We see it as ridiculous because our evaluation of her is not curve based but criteria based and thus objective ('objective' here means 'external and fixed,' and can always be interpreted as a societal or personal invention), so that if this miserable and lowly human were the last person on earth, she would still be miserable and lowly. Indeed, the spiteful person's original assessment of her value as low relative to others' value involved the use of such an objective measure: "They are respected, healthy and unsullied by a venereal disease," she thought, "and I am none of these things. Thus their value and rank are higher than mine." But to render them unhealthy and sullied like herself cannot elevate her if both their value and her value are defined by that objective measure. One who has a scarred face cannot become more beautiful by throwing acid in the face of everyone she meets; all she succeeds in doing is making everyone as ugly as she. Of course, if the world were composed only of people with scarred faces, such faces would perhaps be defined as beautiful, but only because no one would be aware of a more beautiful kind of face. The scarred person in this world, however, does know what an unscarred face looks like, and will never achieve that standard of beauty by making others ugly. Indeed, the more she brings other people down to her level, the less effective she is at changing her perception of her own value, because the act of scarring them is performed so that "they will be low like me." So, with every spiteful act she reminds herself of the objective measure which accords her low value and rank, defeating her attempt to elevate herself.

Malicious and spiteful hatred are my candidates for what Nietzsche called *ressentiment*; they are species of impotent antagonism, con-attitudes positing an objective which cannot be achieved. If my arguments against them are right, one reason why they are wrong (and thus vices) is that they are *irrational*, and this is interesting for two reasons.

First, it has meta-ethical implications. The argument establishes that the moral imperative not to hate (either spitefully or maliciously) is at least a hypothetical imperative (although I will contend later that it is also categorical). Refraining from such hatred doesn't necessitate the sacrifice of a genuine good, and this is a confirmation of Aristotle's contention that one's vicious actions harm oneself, and of Jesus' claim "My yoke is good to bear, my load is light" (Matt. 11:30). When we are called upon to eschew these forms of hatred and revenge, we are not asked to be unreasonably saintly; we are asked to be sensible.

Second, the argument treats these forms of hatred as something we *do*, not something which afflicts us against our will, and it calls upon us to stop. Analyses of the 'passions' (as the derivation of the word suggests) typically make them out to be entities with respect to which we are passive so that we cannot be held responsible for them. But if my analysis is right, even if a certain physical feeling that goes along with malice or spite is something which just afflicts us, these emotions also contain cognitive content over which we have control – for example, the idea that we are in competition for value with a rival – and most important of all, they include a strategy for elevating ourselves. Hence they should be treated as voluntary, and something for which we can be held responsible.[29] By exposing the strategy in these emotions as self-defeating, my hope is to persuade us to stop "doing" malice and spite, if not for others' sake, then for our own.

V. MORAL HATRED AND FORGIVENESS

We have almost finished our analysis of the emotions which stand in the way of genuine forgiveness. We have one more emotion to analyze, and we will then be ready to try to define forgiveness and escape Kolnai's paradox.

Suppose a victim recovers a high degree of belief in her own rank and value. She will thereby overcome resentment, but that emotion will only be replaced by indignation if she

---

29 In this article, "Involuntary Sins," *Philosophical Review*, 94 (January 1985), pp. 3–32, Robert Adams rightly notes that we blame people for emotions such as this, but then concludes that our practice shows that some sins are involuntary. On my view our practice of blaming haters confirms the thesis of the present chapter, namely, that hatred is indeed voluntary.

nonetheless sustains her protest against (but not her personal defense against) the wrongdoing, and this emotion can also block the offer to forgive. Now the word 'indignation' operates like the word 'resentment': it takes as its object actions, not people. I can only be indignant about what you did; I cannot be indignant about you. This semantic practice shows that, like resentment, indignation is an attack on the insulting message in the harmful action (although unlike the resenter's attack, the indignant person's attack is one in which he fully believes). But indignant people often experience a con-attitude towards those who committed the immoral actions, so just as resentment can be linked with one kind of hatred towards the insulter, indignation can be linked with another kind of hatred towards the insulter, which I call *moral hatred*. The indignant person who opposes the message in the insulter's action is expressing aversion for the immoral cause her action promotes, and feels aversion to the insulter herself – her character, her habits, her disposition, or the whole of her – if he takes her, or at least certain components of her, to be thoroughly identified with that cause. Such aversion for her cause and to *her* is motivated by morality; for this reason I have named it 'moral hatred.' It involves believing, by virtue of the insulter's association with the evil cause, that she has "rotted" or "gone bad" so that she now lacks some measure of goodness or moral health.

The name 'moral hatred' is misleading, however, because it suggests that the emotion is always one of virulent opposition, and I want to suggest that it can come in degrees. Moral hatred in the strongest degree is what one would experience towards a Nazi such as Goebbels, who seems irredeemably "rotten" like a piece of meat that has been allowed to become full of maggots and decay.[30] Some of the more frightening mass murderers of our time have prompted the sober judge-

30 I am indebted to Ann Davis for the metaphorical usage of rot in this context, which she developed in a comment on "Rottenness" at a conference on the virtues at the University of San Diego, February 1986. One who judges another to be rotten might believe that the rot can be treated through punishment if it has not spread too far.

ment that they are totally without goodness. No matter how protracted or severe their punishments, how could one even *consider* reconciling oneself with people such as Hitler or Stalin or Charles Manson, who really may not have any decency left in them – nor even any possibility of decency? But rot can come by degrees, and one feels moral aversion to the degree that one judges a person to have rotted. To call a child 'bratty' is to feel a small amount of such aversion to a child who is judged to be in a small way a "rotten kid"; words such as 'cad' or 'jerk,' 'bitch' or 'bastard,' convey graver assessments of the moral state of the person being described, and involve a stronger degree of moral aversion to him or her. And note that even if one thinks that one's wrongdoer retains considerable decency, one might still think he doesn't retain enough of it to make it appropriate to renew certain special relationships such as a marriage or a friendship.

This kind of hatred is not an emotion which aims at bringing a person down some ranking ladder. Of course, the moral hater has a high degree of belief in the evil of the wrongdoer's cause. Hence he believes that there is no need to render the wrongdoer diminished in moral excellence, because he is already convinced of her diminishment in this respect. However, this judgement may coexist with a high degree of respect for her as an *opponent* of the moral cause. The kid who beats up the bully has great respect for him as, among other things, a formidable fighter, which makes him a powerful proponent of the cause against him. When the kid wins the fight over the bully, we cheer him and he is genuinely thrilled at what he has done, precisely because he has achieved victory over someone we all rank highly as an opponent. Indeed, as in any normal competition, moral haters find that the more they respect the hated ones *as* opponents (but perhaps not in any other way), the more they enjoy prevailing over them, especially when their victory is for something as important as morality.[31]

31 I am unclear about exactly what view of the wrongdoer's value moral

The pleasure a moral hater has in seeing his opponent defeated and his own cause victorious can be accompanied by at least two others. If *you* are the one who effected the victory, then in addition to enjoying the thrill of your cause's prevailing you can take pride in the fact that you have accomplished it. And if the victory has to do with combating injustice against *you*, then you can enjoy not only the impersonal benefits that come from the assertion of your moral cause, but also the personal pleasure that comes from the fact that its victory involves the assertion of *you* and your worth. (But you have not pursued your fight in order to get this personal pleasure; it is only a side effect confirming your belief in yourself, albeit a welcome one.) These last two pleasurable feelings are not, admittedly, the noblest feelings in our moral life, but they truly are enjoyable.

You experience none of these pleasures when you hate maliciously or spitefully, because the malice or spite robs you of any genuine victory. Moral hatred can be potent precisely because it can coexist with respect for the opponent throughout the competition. This is not to say that moral haters respect their *opponents'* sense of their own worth as persons; their immoral cause may well involve a vainglorious sense of their status relative to their victim. The kid who beats up the bully enjoys the fact that the bully's puffed-up sense of his own worth has been pricked. It is a pleasure to "take down a peg or two" such an opponent. This is also something that the malicious or spiteful hater might say that he wants – but he understands that objective differently. He wants the literal degradation of his opponent; the moral hater only wants the opponent's false sense of rank and self-worth (his bad *cause*) exposed and defeated, and is delighted when he succeeds. This kind of diminishing action is therefore fully justified.

The isolation and analysis of moral hatred are, I believe,

haters take. Perhaps this depends upon their theory of human worth. Kant's most virulent condemnation of a criminal always presupposes that he is still an end-in-himself; other people may believe that as parts of one's character rot and morally die, one loses value.

critical to the definition of forgiveness. To define forgiveness adequately we must capture the forgiver's change of heart (as distinct from his psychological preparations for it), and analyze it as some kind of absolution from guilt, while still making clear how it is not what Kolnai called condonation.[32] The preceding analysis proposes that the first stage of the forgiving process, namely, the psychological preparation for this change of heart, involves regaining one's confidence in one's own worth despite the immoral action challenging it. This is accomplished by overcoming, in the sense of "giving up" or "repudiating," emotions such as spite or malice, and "overcoming" in the sense of "transcending" resentment. But even after one has overcome these emotions, indignation at the action and some degree of moral hatred towards the wrongdoer may remain. I want to propose that these are the emotions which, when they are overthrown, enable the following change of heart to take place:

The forgiver who previously saw the wrongdoer as someone bad or rotten or morally indecent to some degree has a change of heart when he "washes away" or disregards the wrongdoer's immoral actions or character traits in his ultimate moral judgement of her, and comes to see her as still *decent, not* rotten as a person, and someone with whom he may be able to renew a relationship.

When one has a change of heart towards one's wrongdoer, one "reapproves" of her, so that one is able to consider renewing an association with her. The change of heart is the new understanding of the wrongdoer as a person one can be "for" rather than "against."

So defined, Murphy's conditions for bestowing forgiveness make sense (although I have a few qualms about some of them).[33] Repentance of course provides excellent evidence

32 Kolnai tries to solve the paradox by proposing that forgiveness is the welcoming back of people whose bad actions were the result of subsisting bad character traits, so that when we forgive, we are not condoning their bad actions but forgiving that within them which led them to perform the action. But why doesn't forgiveness of people with bad character traits amount to a condonation of their character?

33 Murphy, in Chapter 1, isolates four situations other than repentance

of the decency of the wrongdoer, and one may also remember something or receive other information to indicate that the wrongdoer is not rotten after all (e.g., past friendship or some extenuating circumstance). And as Murphy's discussion suggests, even if the wrongdoer hasn't separated himself from the immoral cause, forgiving him is warranted if the *forgiveness itself* would effect the separation by softening his hardened heart and thus breaking his rebellion against morality.

Moreover, forgiveness defined in this way is not a response which collapses into renewing relationships according to Kolnai's non-forgiving moral principle: the forgiver does not wait for the wrongdoer to prove himself to be morally reborn in order to reassociate with him. Instead, the forgiver *trusts* that, although he has undergone no rebirth, he is still "good enough" despite what he has done. Forgiveness is thus the decision to see a wrongdoer in a new, more favorable light. Nor is this decision in any way a condonation of wrong. The forgiver never gives up her opposition to the wrongdoer's

in which we might encourage a victim to forgive her wrongdoer: (1) after realizing that the wrongdoer has good motives for the harmful action, (2) after realizing that the wrongdoer has "suffered enough," (3) after the victim has been humiliated, and (4) when the victim has known the wrongdoer for a long time and forgives him "for old times' sake." In each of these situations, argues Murphy, the victim has a way of separating the wrongdoer from his immoral action, so that reaccepting him does not threaten to compromise the victim's self-respect or the rules of the moral order. But I have qualms about three of these criteria. Why should one welcome back someone who has suffered for a long time, or who has been humiliated, if he emerges from his punishment or his humiliation no more decent than when it began? The good motive condition is also problematic: if you realize that your assailant thought he was doing something *good* rather than bad for you, the harm he brought upon you can be said to be a mistake, so that he should really be excused for what he did. And since excusing him is a way of making him innocent of any wrongdoing, one cannot forgive him, because forgiveness, like a pardon, presupposes guilt. Excusing someone and forgiving him are quite different. The "old times' sake" condition fits my analysis, however, because our memories of past friendship can persuade us of the wrongdoer's decency despite the action.

action, nor does she even give up her opposition to the wrongdoer's bad character traits. Instead, she revises her judgement of the person himself – where that person is understood to be something other than or more than the character traits of which she does not approve. And she reaches the *honest* decision that this person does not merit her moral hatred, because he is still decent despite his action. She does not condone something bad by forgiving him, because the forgiveness is precisely the decision that *he* isn't bad (even though his action and the character trait that precipitated it are).

We also have a definition which shows how forgiveness is *directed* at the wrongdoer. When someone bestows forgiveness upon a person, she grants him her approval of him as a person despite what he has done to her. It is therefore natural for her to communicate that approval to the wrongdoer and to seek to renew a relationship with him, although circumstances (e.g., the wrongdoer's death) might make that impossible.[34]

The Old Testament metaphors for forgiveness fit nicely with this definition. If the forgiver "sends away" the moral stain which appeared to be left on the wrongdoer by his action, then she can see him as unstained. If she "lets go" of her sense of herself as the victim of an immoral person, she thereby drops the perspective from which he looks like a morally rotten individual. The one who receives the forgiveness may thus feel cleansed of the stain, cured of the rot, because the forgiver's perspective enables him to see himself as decent rather than (to some degree) corroded or morally damaged. We also have an explanation for the locution "She

---

34 Even if she has this change of heart, the forgiver will not renew a relationship with the wrongdoer if she fears that even though the wrongdoer is still decent within, he has a bad character trait which makes it dangerous for her to resume dealings with him. So a battered wife may forgive her husband, but still seek a divorce on the grounds that she fears his ability to control his violent temper is too low to make it wise for her to remain with him.

forgave him for his _____,'' where the phrase is completed by some immoral action or character trait of the wrongdoer. To forgive someone for an action or a trait is a way of removing it as evidence of the state of his soul, so that one is able to judge him favorably without it. Again, such forgiveness will not be an act of condonation as long as it arises from the forgiver's honest belief that the immoral action does not provide good evidence of the condition of the wrongdoer's soul.

If this analysis is right, forgiveness promises great benefits for both the forgiver and the wrongdoer. It makes possible the benefits that come from a renewed relationship. And it also liberates each of them from the effects of the immoral action itself. The forgiver is no longer trapped in the position of the victim defending herself, and the wrongdoer is no longer in the position of the sinner, stained by sin and indebted to his victim.

But perhaps the greatest good forgiveness can bring is the liberation of the wrongdoer from the effects of the victim's moral hatred. If the wrongdoer fears that the victim is right to see him as cloaked in evil, or as infected with moral rot, these fears can engender moral hatred of himself. Such self-loathing is the feeling that he is, entirely or in part, morally hideous, unclean, infected. It can be directed at his character or dispositions or, more dangerously, towards everything that he is, so that he comes to believe that there is nothing good or decent in him. If it is directed only towards a part of himself which he believes can be made better, it may have desirable moral effects; but if it is directed at central components of himself which he thinks cannot be changed, or at everything he is, it can lead to self-destruction. (But to the extent that a bad person does feel this emotion, doesn't this show he isn't entirely evil? Hating yourself as evil seems to show that part of you is siding with morality.)

Those who morally hate themselves seek to forgive themselves. It is interesting that both Judaism and Christianity regard self-forgiveness as hard, frequently representing it as accomplished through the receiving of forgiveness from God – a forgiveness which communicates to the wrongdoer that despite what he has done he is still "of worth" and, in particular, valuable enough to be liked and regarded as a "decent thing" which is capable of change for the better. This is something he might find it difficult to convince himself of if he is struck by the horror of his own deeds. But a victim's forgiveness of his wrongdoer can communicate the same message, so that the wrongdoer may reason, "If he can see enough in me to welcome me back, then maybe I am not such a hideous person after all." This might be the first step towards coming to like himself again and renewing a commitment to morality. So there is a considerable benefit which forgiveness may bring: It may enable wrongdoers to forgive themselves by showing them that there is still enough decency in them to warrant renewed association with them. It may save them from the hell of self-loathing.

Given the good such forgiveness can effect, this definition may provide grounds for refuting Murphy's provocative proposal that forgiveness may sometimes be a bad thing. But the definition also raises a second question, which Murphy does not discuss: I have represented the forgiver as one whose change of heart is based on an honest reassessment of the decency of the wrongdoer, and it seems that such forgiveness cannot be "willed" if one is convinced of the opposite. Yet we are enjoined to forgive those who wrong us. Given that it is self-defeating to try to will to believe anything, how can this injunction make sense? Even if I am right that we have the capacity to control and stop emotions such as hatred, how can we control our beliefs about another person's decency? Should we even want to do so? Moreover, by sometimes speaking of the forgiver's change of heart as the "decision" to see someone in a new light, have I confused a genuine change of heart with the mere *attempt* at such a change, which might be all that the injunction to forgive requires of us?

I will pursue these questions in Chapter 4. But for now, I will stop, and await Murphy's reactions to the analysis thus far given.

Chapter 3

Hatred: a qualified defense

JEFFRIE MURPHY

It's great to be back in Chicago where people still
know how to hate.
Mike Royko, on returning home after covering
the 1972 Democratic Convention in
San Francisco

Jean Hampton distinguishes three kinds of hatred: simple
hatred, moral hatred, and malicious-spiteful hatred
(Nietzsche's *ressentiment*).[1] Simply having an aversion to
someone because of some non-morally objectionable quality
(e.g., he is a bore) is unavoidable and raises no moral issues
unless one acts on the feeling in immoral ways. (Trying to
avoid a bore at a party is permissible; killing the bore –
though very tempting – is not.) Moral hatred is aversion to a
person (e.g., a Nazi) because of the immoral cause with
which he is identified, and is coupled with a desire to triumph over him and his cause. There is no desire to hurt the
person *simpliciter* but only a willingness to allow such hurt if
unavoidable in the pursuit of victory over his immoral cause.
Malicious or spiteful hatred, however, has as its very object
the attempt to diminish and hurt another and thereby gain
competitive advantage over him and his status; and it is this
kind of hatred, argues Hampton, that is both irrational and
immoral.

I am inclined to agree with almost everything Hampton

1 Chapter 2, "Forgiveness, Resentment and Hatred."

says – as far as it goes. However, there is, in my view, an important dimension of hatred that Hampton does not explore – a dimension that in some way combines elements of her categories of moral and malicious hatred and thus suggests that the moral phenomenology of hatred and resentment is even more complicated than her already very complex analysis indicates. Or so I shall argue.

The desire to hurt another, to bring him low, is not – in my judgment – always motivated by the competitive desire to appear better than that person in some way. Sometimes, I suggest, such a desire is motivated by feelings that are at least partly *retributive* in nature – e.g., feelings that another person's current level of well-being is undeserved or ill-gotten (perhaps at one's own expense) and that a reduction in that well-being will simply represent his getting his just deserts. (This is no doubt the thought behind the old common law principle that no man shall be allowed to profit from his own wrongdoing.) Take a case where Jones has injured me, has taken unfair advantage of me, has brought me low, and is himself unrepentant and flourishing. I hate him and want him brought low. My attitude here is like Hampton's spiteful hatred in that I want Jones to be hurt. But it is like her moral hatred in that part of the basis for desiring the hurt is the desire to restore what seems (at least to me) to be the proper moral balance of whatever goods are in question, and not a simple desire to look better than Jones on some morally irrelevant scale of comparison. It is not the kind of hatred felt by Saul for David (David inflicted no unjust injury on Saul) but is a kind that might be felt, for example, by former inmates of a concentration camp toward a former camp commandant finally captured and put on trial for crimes against humanity, or by American soldiers now dying of cancer toward those who recklessly exposed them to radiation during atomic testing, or – on a less global scale – by a man toward his wife and his best friend when he discovers that they have betrayed him and have been conducting an adulterous affair behind his back, or by a woman toward a rapist whose attack has left her forever terrified and sexually insecure. The hatred felt by such persons will typically have a *righteous* dimension – indicated by the fact that they, unlike people motivated by petty envy or spite, are often willing to avow publicly, as appropriate and as nothing to be ashamed of, the true nature of their feelings and motives. Such people often show up, for example, at criminal sentencing hearings where, as crime victims, they want to influence the judge to impose very harsh treatment on those who have harmed them – sometimes ruined their lives utterly. Even those who would argue that such appeals should not influence a judge must surely admit that the desires represented in the appeals are in some sense understandable, natural, and appropriate to the harm done to those people – that they involve something which is, even if not ultimately authoritative, at least more worthy than petty spite or envy of our attention and respect. I shall call the hatred present in such cases "retributive hatred" and shall suggest that, although in most cases it should be overcome, it still deserves a certain amount of respect. It is not obviously irrational or immoral. Indeed, it is sometimes both therapeutic for the victim and appropriately directed toward the wrongdoer and is not to be dismissed with a few pious clichés.

It is striking the degree to which those who wish to give hatred a bad name tend to focus on examples either of hatred that is not retributive or of retributive hatred that is clearly unjustified because the person hated is in fact (the hater's beliefs to the contrary) not really guilty of any unjust conduct. Hampton's example of David and Saul is of the former sort, as is her example of the mother who is above hatred and resentment of her child. (David did no wrong to Saul, and the child was not guilty of *responsible* wrongdoing.) An example of the latter sort is provided in the following passage from Simone Weil's *Gravity and Grace* (once quoted by Herbert Morris in protest against my sympathies for resentment and hatred):[2]

---

2 Herbert Morris was the commentator when I presented a version of Chapter 1 at a symposium at the 1987 meetings of the American

A beloved being who disappoints me. I have written to him. It is impossible that he should not reply by saying what I have said to myself in his name. Men owe us what we imagine they will give us. We must forgive them this debt. To accept the fact that they are other than the creatures of our imagination is to imitate the renunciation of God. I also am other than what I imagine myself to be. To know this is forgiveness.

This is a dark passage, but I take it that at least a part of Weil's point is this: Because of our pride, our vanity, our self-importance, we often project upon the world an illusion of what others owe us and thus quite improperly feel ourselves wronged when those others act in ways contrary to the illu-sion we have created. To this observation, I am inclined to reply as follows: *Of course* people sometimes fantasize hurts, and *of course* any hatred based on such imaginary injuries is totally unjustified – both irrational and immoral – but are we to conclude from this that there are no *real* moral injuries the perpetrators of which are quite rightly to be resented or even hated?

Surely the answer to this question is a clear *no*. If a total case is to be made against hatred, it must be made against examples where the hatred appears at its best and most *prima facie* justified – examples where a person has in fact been treated very immorally, has been hurt badly by the immoral treatment, reasonably believes that the wrongdoer is totally unrepentant of the wrongdoing and is in fact living a life of freedom and contentment,[3] and – *given all that* – hates the wrongdoer and desires that the wrongdoer suffer. Such

---

Philosophical Association, Pacific Division. Some of the thoughts in the present chapter have been developed in response to his provocative remarks. My paper, Morris's comments, and a rejoinder by me will appear in a forthcoming issue of *Criminal Justice Ethics*.

3 Let us suppose that the wrongdoer's contentment is comparable to that enjoyed by the victim prior to the wrongdoing but is now considerably greater than that enjoyed by the victim, who has been plunged into misery by the wrongdoing. To make the case as compelling as possible, let us also suppose that the wrongdoer's current level of well-being is a direct consequence of his wrongdoing.

cases may be rare, but – confessing that I firmly hold the unmodern view that there is such a thing as evil in this world – I believe that they do exist. For example, when the victims in a recent series of vicious rapes in Phoenix testified that they wanted the "Camelback rapist," who had utterly trashed the lives of some of them, to be sentenced to the maximum term that the law allowed, many of them openly admitted that they were acting out of anger and hatred.[4] These women were outraged at the thought that this vicious man, utterly unrepentant, could soon continue to lead a free life, given what he had done to their lives. I sympathized with their anger and hatred, having no inclination at all to call them petty or spiteful. I would have found it indecently insensitive and presumptuous had anyone charged them with the vice of failing to forgive and love their enemies or had anyone read them passages from Simone Weil on the tendency of human beings to imagine wrongs where there are no real wrongs – had, in short, anyone attempted to add to their already considerable burdens by making them feel guilty or ashamed over a reaction that was, given what was done to them, natural, fitting, and proper. My feelings (and theirs) in such a case may be subject to criticism, but of one thing I am sure: *This* is the kind of case that must be discussed and made central in any comprehensive attack on the nature and justification of hatred, the kind of hatred I have called retributive in nature.[5]

---

4 E. J. Montini, "Victims of 'Camelback Rapist' Pour Out Anger, Fear and Sadness," *Arizona Republic*, May 12, 1987, page A2. (The word "Camelback" in this context refers to a region of the city of Phoenix.)
5 It is common these days to hear the complaint that our society – particularly our legal system – is callous toward the victims of crime. One example of such callousness may be a refusal to respect the natural feelings of hatred that some victims may feel toward those who have harmed them – feelings that perhaps deserve more respect than simply being dismissed as irrelevant because "merely vindictive." There is – for reasons to be explored later – social and personal danger latent in such powerful feelings, but such danger might be minimized if these feelings – instead of being ignored – are institutionalized. (Athena, remember, did not banish the Furies. Rather she made an honorable home for them in Athens where, though constrained by process, they

Hatred: a qualified defense

Resentment, I have previously argued, is essentially tied to self-respect. It is an emotional defense against attacks on self-esteem and thus is, as both Nietzsche and Hampton suggest, a sign of weakness; for if one is certain of the value of one's self, it will not be truly threatened by attack from another and will not stand in need of defense. But of course one is never certain of such matters, and thus some weakness or vulnerability in the area of self-esteem seems to me an ineliminable part of the human condition. We are, at least in part, social and socialized products – creatures whose sense of self is so much a part of our social setting that the idea of self-respect or self-esteem cannot be totally detached from a concern with how others (some others) regard and treat us, for "men always consider the sentiments of others in their judgments of themselves."[6] To think otherwise is to fall victim to the liberal myth of atomic individualism in its crudest form. A truly

could still speak for victims and express their legitimate outrage over wrongdoing.) Allowing victims some advisory role in criminal sentencing thus might be a legal practice that benefits both the community and the victims themselves; for the practice recognizes the validity of the hatred while placing important constraints on its excess. As such, it might even help to educate persons on the legitimate bounds of hatred. Of course, we hear much talk about crimes being offenses against the state or community as a whole – against the general rules of order in which all citizens have an equal stake. Because of this, it is often thought that all citizens have the same stake in demanding punishment for crime and that individual victims, therefore, should play no special role. But this is too simplistic. The rapist may be a free rider on the legal compliance of all of us, but only some very unfortunate subset of us suffer from him in ways that seriously undermine our actual well-being. This is revealed in the fact that most crimes are also torts; and the only person who can sue in tort is (normally) the true victim who is actually hurt and not every law-abiding citizen. Is it wrong for a person to pursue a tort suit out of retributive hatred? Or suppose a victim gets to see the person who wronged him suffer what he takes to be an appropriate harm – not through any agency of the victim but simply through luck. Must he, if a virtuous person, feel guilty or ashamed if he takes some pleasure in witnessing this? Must one feel guilty even over pleasing *fantasies* of revenge?

6   David Hume, *A Treatise of Human Nature* (1739–40), Book II, Part I, Section VIII. See also John Rawls's discussion of the social nature of the primary good of self-respect in *A Theory of Justice* (Cambridge, Mass.: Harvard University Press, 1971), pp. 440–6.

strong person will have the resources to fight off attacks on his self-esteem when they are unjustified, but no person is so "strong" (so asocial) as to be totally indifferent to all such attacks – so indifferent that he does not even resent them.[7] Hampton reminds us that Jesus set an example that it is possible to be otherwise, but Jesus – being divine – perhaps had certain advantages that mere mortals lack. It may not be too difficult to ignore insults and injuries from mere human beings if one, being the Son of God, has a rather more impressive reference class from which to draw one's self-esteem.[8]

Even supposing that what I have said about resentment is correct, however, it may not seem that it will help very much in mounting a case for the justification of hatred – even retributive hatred. For the hater, unlike the resenter, is not simply engaged in protest and self-assertion. He also desires that the object of his hate be *hurt*. If hate is sometimes justified, then the desire to hurt another must sometimes be justified. But how can this be?

This is how: If it is morally permissible intentionally to do X (under a certain description), then it is surely permissible to *desire* to do X (under the same description). If there is any truth at all in retributive theories of punishment, then it is sometimes permissible that persons be hurt (punishment hurts) in response to their wrongdoing. It is thus sometimes permissible to hurt people for retributive reasons. Given this, it is sometimes permissible to desire to hurt people for retrib-

7 In John Irving's novel *The Hotel New Hampshire*, the character Franny attempts to deal with her trauma as a gang-rape victim by continually telling herself that the rape never touched "the me in me." She never achieves any real peace, however, until she manages to get at least partial revenge against the gang's leader. Her inherent decency prevents her from getting total revenge, however, as decency has a way of doing – a theme I shall explore later in this chapter.

8 The use of a divinity as a moral model raises problems analogous to those raised by Cartesian dualism on the mind-body problem. The more a divinity is made to appear like a human being, the less divine the being appears. The more the being is made to appear genuinely different from human beings, however, the less clear it is how the being can be copied or used as an ideal or model by mere human beings.

utive reasons. Using Hampton's idea that desires or emotions are strategies, we may say that retributive hatred is a
strategy designed to see (and to let the victim see) that people
get their just deserts; as such it is neither irrational nor
immoral. The wrongdoer gets his just deserts (and what is
wrong with that?), and the victim gets some personal satisfaction from seeing the justice done (and what is wrong with
that?). Deterrence values may also be served, for a person
perceived as given to hatred and revenge is perhaps less
likely to become a victim than are those who are not given to
such passions. ("I'm Noko Marie, don't mess with me!" says
a vindictive Kliban cat.)[9] Retributive hatred is thus in principle vindicated as a permissible, if not mandatory, response of
a victim to wrongdoing.[10]

9 If reciprocal altruism is an adaptive evolutionary strategy, then it
   would seem that reciprocal hatred might be as well. In this sense
   hatred will properly be called a *natural* response to certain kinds of
   wrongdoing. On the evolutionary advantages of a strategy of "tit for
   tat," see Robert Axelrod, *The Evolution of Cooperation* (New York: Basic
   Books, 1984).
10 The retributive theory of punishment is, in essence, the theory that
   people are to suffer punishment because they *deserve* it and not simply
   because social utility (e.g., crime deterrence) requires it. Critics often
   describe retribution as an obviously *pointless* infliction of suffering – as
   though future deterrence clearly has a point whereas redressing an
   injustice does not. But this would surely need to be argued for; as it
   stands, it is simply question begging. The retributive theory of punishment is, of course, controversial, and the complex arguments pro and
   con on the matter cannot be surveyed in the present context.
   Attempting to follow in the footsteps of Kant, I have in the past written
   extensively in defense of retribution's essential connection to some of
   our most basic moral ideas – our ideas of justice and fairness and our
   conception of people as morally significant in part because they are
   capable of the kind of responsible wrongdoing for which blame and
   punishment are appropriate (as they are capable of responsible
   rightdoing for which praise and reward are appropriate). I cannot possibly rehearse here the case I have attempted to develop in the past in
   defense of retributivism, and so I must simply content myself with
   referring the reader to my earlier writings – specifically my collection
   of essays *Retribution, Justice, and Therapy: Essays in the Philosophy of Law*
   (Dordrecht: Reidel, 1979).
      In my view, the most persuasive brief presentations of retributive
   thinking are to be found in Herbert Morris's essay "Persons and
   Punishment," *The Monist*, 52 (October 1968), pp. 475–501, and Peter

Does this mean that we should all enter at full speed the wide and wonderful world of hatred – cultivating and nursing it in ourselves and teaching it to our children? I think not. Thus, having made the best case I can in favor of hatred, I shall now begin to consider what is wrong with it – why it perhaps deserves much of the bad press it has received and why, in general, we should seek to overcome it.

Note that what I have attempted to show thus far is that, in a certain restricted class of cases (cases of retribution), hatred is *in principle* vindicated or justified. But showing that some response is in principle justified does not by itself show that the response is ever *in fact* justified, *all* relevant things considered; for to justify in principle is to justify for a pure and clear case, and it is always possible that the world never contains a pure or clear case – or that we are never in a position to *know* if we are confronted with one. Given such a state of the world, it thus might always be a bad *policy* to exhibit the response, no matter how justified it may be in principle.[11]

Strawson's essay "Freedom and Resentment," *Proceedings of the British Academy*, 1962. Also to be recommended is Herbert Fingarette's presidential address "Punishment and Suffering," *Proceedings of the American Philosophical Association*, 1977, where he pursues the idea that a "humbling of the will" is essential to punishment. Michael S. Moore's valuable essay "The Moral Worth of Retribution" appeared as this book was in press. (See Chapter 8 of *Responsibility, Character, and the Emotions: New Essays in Moral Psychology*, ed. Ferdinand Schoeman (Cambridge University Press, 1987), pp. 179–219.)

Both Morris and I have recently expressed some doubts about retributivism as the sole and unqualified response to criminal wrongdoing. See Herbert Morris, "A Paternalistic Theory of Punishment," *American Philosophical Quarterly*, 18 (October 1981), pp. 263–71 and my "Retributivism, Moral Education, and the Liberal State," *Criminal Justice Ethics*, 4 (Winter-Spring 1985), pp. 3–11. See also my "Does Kant Have a Theory of Punishment?" 87 *Columbia Law Review*, no. 3 (April 1987), pp. 509–32.

11 Many people argue in this way with respect to the issue of capital punishment. It is consistent to believe that there is nothing wrong in principle with executing people for certain kinds of crimes and yet to oppose capital punishment, even for persons convicted of those crimes, on the grounds that legal trials are too error prone to guarantee that the punishment will fall only on those who are truly guilty and who truly deserve it.

Hatred: a qualified defense

With this pattern of thought in mind, consider what Kant, a staunch defender of a retributive outlook on punishment, says about hatred and revenge in his *Metaphysical Elements of Virtue*:

> It is . . . a duty of virtue not only to refrain from repaying another's enmity with hatred out of mere revenge but also never even to call upon the world-judge for vengeance – partly because man has enough guilt of his own to be greatly in need of forgiveness and partly, and indeed especially, because no punishment, no matter from whom it comes, may be inflicted out of hatred. Hence men have a duty to cultivate a *conciliatory spirit (placabilitas)*. But this must not be confused with *placid toleration* of injuries *(mitis iniuriarum patientia)*, renunciation of the rigorous means *(rigorosa)* for preventing the recurrence of injuries by other men. (Gregor translation, p. 130)

Consider also a couple of related passages from his *Religion within the Limits of Reason Alone*:

> We call a man evil, however, not because he performs actions that are evil (contrary to law) but because these actions are of such a nature that we may infer from them the presence in him of evil maxims. In and through experience we can observe actions contrary to law, and we can observe (at least in ourselves) that they are performed in the consciousness that they are unlawful; but a man's maxims, sometimes even his own, are not thus observable; consequently the judgment that the agent is an evil man cannot be made with certainty if grounded on experience. (Green and Hudson translation, p. 16)

> [People] may picture themselves as meritorious, feeling themselves guilty of no such offenses as they see others burdened with; nor do they ever inquire whether good luck should not have the credit, or whether by reason of the cast of mind which they could discover, if they only would, in their own inmost nature, they would have practiced similar vices, had not inability, temperament, training, and circumstances of time and place which serve to tempt one (matters which are not imputable) kept them out of the way of those vices. This dishonesty,

by which we humbug ourselves and which thwarts the establishing of a true moral disposition in us, extends itself outwardly also to falsehood and deception of others. If this is not
to be termed wickedness, it at least deserves the name of
worthlessness, and is an element in the radical evil of human
nature, which (inasmuch as it puts out of tune the moral capacity to judge what a man is to be taken for, and renders wholly
uncertain both internal and external attribution of responsibility) constitutes the foul taint in our race. (pp. 33–4)

There is much that is puzzling in these passages, but in general they can be read as commentaries upon two well-known
Christian teachings: "Vengeance is mine; I will repay, saith
the Lord" (Rom. 12:19) and "Let him who is without sin cast
the first stone" (John 8:7).[12] For Kant here seems to be making two main objections to hatred and to any action – even
punishment – motivated by hatred:

1. Human beings, given their cognitive limitations, are
never in a position to know if another (whose essential character is, after all, inner) is evil to the degree that hatred of him
would be justified. Such matters are properly left to God who
"knows the heart."[13]

2. Each human being is himself so morally flawed as to lack

12 I have always quoted the passage from John, as I do here, in the form
   in which I remember it from my childhood – when scriptural readings
   were always claimed to be from the King James Version. I was thus
   very surprised when I was recently informed that the passage in the
   King James Version actually appears in what strikes me as a less ele-
   gant form: "He that is without sin among you, let him first cast a stone
   at her." Perhaps my religious memories are derived from Hollywood
   biblical epics.
13 Kant (*Religion*, pp. 60–1) speaks of God as being uniquely qualified to
   make ultimate judgment because He "knows the heart" of the wrongdoer – a theme whose implications I pursue more fully in my "Does
   Kant Have a Theory of Punishment?" The idea that God is a being
   uniquely able and qualified to assign suffering in proper proportion to
   moral iniquity plays a crucial role in Kant's famous "moral proof" for
   the existence of God. Note that if hatred and vengeance are permissible for God, then there must be a sense in which these responses are
   in principle permissible. Note also that the passage from Rom. 12:19, far
   from being an argument against the desire for vengeance, is a *promise*
   of vengeance.

proper standing to hate and despise other human beings and to seek to hurt or destroy them. If any human being is to be utterly banished from the realm of benevolent concern (as hate would so banish), then only a morally superior being, God, is in a position to take such a stand.

Both of these arguments are ways of raising the question, Who are *we* to judge and thus to hate? (Given how little we know and how morally flawed we are, is it not presumptuous of us to judge and hate? Is this not a clear example of self-deception and a sin of arrogance or pride?) In my view, neither of the arguments is conclusive as it stands, and yet there is a profound *caution* against hatred being expressed in each. Let me try to indicate what this may be.

Do we know enough to hate? Kant claims that we can never know for certain if another being is truly evil; for his acts may be motivated for reasons (perhaps honorable, perhaps insane) that do not come to light – *cannot* come to light if Kant's metaphysical view that moral motivation lies in a non-physical noumenal realm is correct. Suppose we grant this. What lesson are we meant to learn – that we should never judge or condemn others at all, that we should never have criminal trials, that we should open the doors of all the jails? Surely such a response would be drastic and irrational, and Kant himself never suggests it. Although we may not have knowledge (in the sense of Cartesian certainty) of human evil and responsibility, we surely are able to form *reasonable beliefs* about such matters and surely are sometimes justified when we act on such beliefs. If we waited for Cartesian certainty, we would never act at all – in any area of our life. And this would be suicidal – both socially and personally.

What then is the point of Kant's epistemological caution against hatred? I think it is this: Even though the necessities of maintaining civilized life and schemes of just cooperation require that we sometimes make and act on our best judgments of wrongdoing and responsibility (that we have trials and jails, in short), we should be very cautious about over-dramatizing and overmoralizing what we must (regretfully) do here by portraying it as some righteous cosmic drama – as a holy war against ultimate sin and evil. Such a view would, among other things, tempt us to dangerous excesses – excesses that would harm others through our oversevere (and thus unjust) treatment of them and harm us through our own corruption – as one is always corrupted if one presumes to play God. We should always be vividly aware of our limitations as human beings – and never more so than in cases where we can do great evil if we are not aware. Such a caution is particularly appropriate when directed toward one who is (or believes he is) a *victim* of wrongdoing. For such persons (as Simone Weil noted) have a natural tendency to make hasty judgments of responsibility, magnify the wrong done to them, and thus seek retribution out of all just proportion to what is actually appropriate. (This insight into human nature lies behind the old common law maxim that a man is not to be a judge in any controversy to which he is a party.) People sometimes get such matters exactly right; but, more typically, they get them wrong – more and more wrong the more wildly angry and filled with hatred they become. Because of this lesson in humility, cautions against hatred and actions motivated out of hatred are surely in order.[14]

Are we pure enough to hate? Kant is not concerned merely to make the epistemological point that victims, being interested parties, may have their perceptions and judgments too clouded to be reliable haters. He also seeks to raise this *moral* caution against hatred: Even if it were possible to be absolutely sure of the iniquity of another person, possible to know exactly how much suffering his evil deserves, no one of us is sufficiently better than that person to be qualified to

14 As argued previously, it might be desirable to allow crime victims some advisory role, constrained by process, in criminal sentencing. But would we want them to have the final authority on such matters? It is one thing to advocate some institutionally constrained role for the hatred and anger that crime victims quite naturally feel; it is quite another thing to open the door to vigilante self-help in the realm of retribution.

demand or inflict the suffering. If a stone may be cast only by the morally pure, none of us can ever – without hypocrisy or self-deception – cast a stone.

But is this a genuine obstacle to all hating – to all desires to inflict retributive hurt? Suppose I hate Jones because he has spitefully damaged my favorite piece in my art collection, and I want to see him suffer for having done this. I pause and consider the principle "Let him who is without sin cast the first stone," note accurately that I have never spitefully damaged anyone's favorite possession, and thus feel perfectly free to cast away. I am not morally perfect, of course, for I have in my time done several unnice things – suppose, for example, I once committed adultery. But how could this be relevant here – given that the occasion of my present hatred is what Jones did to my treasure and not anything about his sex life? Given that I am totally innocent ("without sin") with respect to the kinds of wrongs germane to the present case, may I not thus indulge my retributive hatred without any fear that I am a hypocrite or am engaged in self-deception? Are not both Jesus and Kant adequately answered by such a process of reflection?

I think not. The above response is too shallow, for it fails to reflect the kind of serious moral introspection that Jesus and Kant are attempting to provoke. The point is not to deny that many people lead lives that are both legally and morally correct. The point is rather to force such people to face honestly the question of *why* they have lived in such a way. Is it (as they would no doubt like to believe) because their inner characters manifest true integrity and are thus morally superior to those of people whose behavior has been less exemplary? Or is it, at least in part, a matter of what John Rawls has called "luck on the natural and social lottery?"[15] Perhaps, as Kant suggests, their favored upbringing and social circumstances, or the fact that they have never been placed in situations where they have been similarly tempted, or their fear of being found out has had considerably more to

15 See John Rawls, *A Theory of Justice*, pp. 65–75.

do with their compliance with the rules of law and morality than they would like to admit. Perhaps if they imagined themselves possessed of Gyges' ring (a ring which, in Plato's myth in *Republic*, makes its wearer invisible), they would – if honest with themselves – have to admit that they would probably use the ring, not to perform anonymous acts of charity, but to perform some acts of considerable evil – acts comparable, perhaps, to the acts for which they often hate others. If they follow through honestly on this process of self-examination, they will have learned another important lesson in moral humility.

One does not, of course, want to let natural-lottery arguments carry one too far down this road of moral humility, for an utter absorption in such considerations would spell the end of moral responsibility and the moral significance of human beings that is founded upon such responsibility – would, indeed, spell the end of one's own moral significance. Does not each person want to believe of himself, as a part of his pride in his human dignity, that he is *capable* of performing, freely and responsibly performing, evil acts that would quite properly earn for him the retributive hatred of others? And should he not at least sometimes extend this compliment to them?[16] Camus expresses this concern forcefully:

> I do not believe . . . that there is no responsibility in this world and that we must give way to that modern tendency to absolve everyone, victim and murderer, in the same confusion. Sentimental confusion is made up of cowardice rather than generosity and eventually justifies whatever is worst in this world. If you keep on excusing, you eventually give your blessing to the slave camp, to cowardly force, to organized execu-

16 In Friedrich Dürrenmatt's novel *Traps*, Alfredo Traps derives enormous feelings of agency and pride when he is persuaded at a mock trial that he has performed, with full moral responsibility, an evil act. He has never had such feelings before but has always simply regarded himself as a "helpless victim of the age." He thus resists (to the point of executing himself!) all attempts to argue that he was not responsible and thus should not be hated and punished.

tions, to the cynicism of the great political monsters: you finally hand over your brothers. This can be seen around us. But it so happens, in the present state of the world, that the man of today wants laws and institutions suitable to a convalescent.[17]

The lessons of moral humility are thus not to be regarded as fatal objections to all hatred in all cases, and that is why I have referred to them as *cautions*. But they are deeply important cautions. They should make all morally reflective persons pause and at least think twice about their hatreds and the courses of action on which these hatreds tempt them to embark. For to commit to a strategy of retributive hatred is to take on strong assumptions of moral epistemology and moral qualifications – assumptions that may prove insupportable. If they do, then one's hatreds, however motivated initially by a righteous desire to defend one's moral worth against assault, will have in fact accomplished nothing but a diminishing of that worth. This would leave one open to *self-hatred* – an outcome that any rational strategy would surely seek to avoid.

Considering retributive hatred as a strategy, as Hampton insightfully invites us so to consider all emotions, additional cautions against it emerge. If retributive hatred involves a desire to hurt others in a way comparable to the hurt they have inflicted, then one who is driven by such hatred will remain unfulfilled until the retributive hurt is in fact inflicted. But there are often serious (sometimes fatal) obstacles in the way of such an occurrence; and thus the hatred, deprived of

17 Albert Camus, "Reflections on the Guillotine," in *Resistance, Rebellion, and Death*, trans. Justin O'Brien (New York: Knopf, 1961), pp. 230–1. When we take the position of spectator on the world in which we live, we are tempted by the maxim "To understand all is to forgive all." When we are actively engaged as agents in our world, however, we cannot accept this maxim, for it seems to spell the end of human moral significance and the moral relations that we value with other people. For an argument that both perspectives are unavoidable and that human beings must thus live perpetually in the tension between them, see Thomas Nagel, *The View from Nowhere* (New York: Oxford University Press, 1986). See also Lewis White Beck, *The Actor and the Spectator* (New Haven, Conn.: Yale University Press, 1975).

an outlet, begins to poison a person from within. (An appreciation of the self-destructive potential of hatred and resentment, deprived of an outlet and thus forced into sublimation, was one of Nietzsche's great insights.)[18] We speak of people who "nurse a grudge" and often regard them with a mixture of contempt and pity. But people would not have to nurse their grudges if they would simply act them out – get even – and one may well wonder why they do not simply do this and get the poison out of their systems.

There are, I think, three reasons why persons may sometimes fail to act out their retributive hatreds.

1. It is impossible to get even. The person you hate may be protected and unreachable or may be indifferent to whatever evil you might seek to inflict on him. Or it may for some other reason be impossible to inflict upon him exactly what you think he deserves, and you might be unable to calculate a proper equivalent. (Hegel, in what in another writer might be taken for humor, asks how we are to exact an eye for an eye and a tooth for a tooth if we are dealing with an eyeless and toothless destroyer of eyes and teeth.) Perhaps the evil of your enemy is of such magnitude that no punishment you could inflict would seem properly proportional. Or your enemy might even be dead. Thus nothing you could do would ever count, in fact or in your eyes, as your getting even with him. Here we have impotent hatred – an emotional state that is potentially, as Nietzsche argued, very self-destructive.

2. It is too costly to get even. Spinoza, in writing of the fear of death, does not argue that it is irrational to fear death. He

18 "The slave revolt in morality begins when *ressentiment* itself becomes creative and gives birth to values: the *ressentiment* of natures that are denied true reaction, that of deeds, and compensate themselves with an imaginary revenge. . . . *Ressentiment* itself, if it should appear in the noble man, consummates and exhausts itself in an immediate reaction, and therefore does not *poison*." Friedrich Nietzsche, *On the Genealogy of Morals*, Essay I, Section 10 (pp. 36 and 39 of the Walter Kaufmann translation; New York: Random House, 1967).

argues rather that it is irrational to be *led* by this fear. His central idea, relevant to many emotions, is that a rational person will apply a kind of cost-benefit analysis to his mental life and will not pursue any passion to the extent that he loses more than he gains in the satisfaction of that passion. How absurd, argues Spinoza, if one becomes so consumed by the fear of death that one misses out on the many joys and positive benefits life offers. And thus he writes:

> A free man, that is to say, a man who lives according to the dictates of reason alone, is not led by fear of death, but directly desires the good, that is to say, desires to act, to live, and to preserve his being in accordance with the principle of seeking his own profit. He thinks, therefore, of nothing less than death, and his wisdom is a meditation upon life.[19]

So too for hatred. Imagine the costs in time and trouble (and perhaps liberty if illegal means are required and perhaps safety if your enemy is powerful or has powerful friends) that might be involved in planning revenge, tracking down, and then adequately harming the object of one's hatred. It could, in some cases, become one's life instead of being a part of one's life; and the hater would pay a price for being led by this passion comparable to the one Spinoza warns against with respect to the fear of death. Lucky indeed the person for whom the legal system will institutionalize a portion of these feelings. For feelings of hatred can, in many cases, consume one's entire self.[20] Thus it might be seen a blessing – perhaps

19 *Ethics*, Four, LXVII. I have explored this thought in some detail in my "Rationality and the Fear of Death," *The Monist*, 59 (April 1976) pp. 187–203, and reprinted in my *Retribution, Justice, and Therapy*.
20 Fay Weldon's novel *The Life and Loves of a She-Devil* is the best portrayal I know of both the charms and dangers of retributive and other hatreds. Ruth, the central character, driven by hatred and desire for revenge, takes extraordinary steps (including reconstructive surgery and a general change of her very identity) to bring her enemies (her former husband and his new wife) low. When it is all over, she has brought them as low as she had ever desired. But, given the costs she has borne, it is unclear that she emerges a winner. Some of her hatreds also seem to be in Hampton's category of malicious hatreds and illus-

even divine grace – to have the burden of hatred lifted from one's mind. For this reason forgiveness can bless the forgiver as much as or more than it blesses the one forgiven.[21]

3. *Moral decency imposes constraints.* Suppose that, in a particular case, you know you can pursue hatred and revenge without incurring any of the previously noted costs. Suppose you have your enemy totally in your power, can inflict upon him exactly what you think he deserves, and can do so with impunity. Suppose you even know the degree of his guilt and exactly what suffering he deserves, and further suppose you know that, even with Gyges' ring, you would never have committed the wrong for which your enemy now stands hated. Such a case is perhaps impossible in the real world, but let us suppose as a thought experiment that you find yourself presented with one. Is this at last a case where no cautions apply and where hatred and revenge may be freely and happily indulged?

Even here I have doubts. Sometimes it will seem that the only adequate (i.e., proportional) punishment for the evil a person has done requires that one, in inflicting the punish-

> trate Hampton's important point that the strategy of malicious hatred is irrational because, the moment it accomplishes its aim of bringing another low, it makes it impossible to take any competitive pride or satisfaction in being superior to such a low person. Ruth's case may simply illustrate the fact that sometimes the worst thing that can happen to us is to get what we want.
>
> Hatreds can also provoke endless and continually escalating feuds – another heavy cost to consider. See Thomas Berger's novel *Feud* and, of course, Aeschylus's *Oresteia*.
>
> 21 Some of Herbert Morris's remarks forced me to think about the ways in which forgiveness benefits the forgiver as well as the one forgiven. When I first wrote on forgiveness (see Chapter 1), I was inclined to dismiss its effects on the forgiver as morally irrelevant – as matters of mere prudence, self-interest, or mental health. I now see that this was a mistake. Surely a legitimate concern of morality is with virtue or personal excellence – one's attempt to mold the object that is *oneself* into the best and most admirable instance of humanity of which one is capable. (The task of virtue makes one into an artist with oneself as the work of art.) The elimination of self-destructive or self-limiting passions will surely be an important part of such a project.

ment, perform an act one finds intrinsically immoral; and thus one will balk at its performance even under the banner of just retribution. For example, there is a sense in which it seems that the only punishment adequate for a torturer and mutilator is torture and mutilation, and yet one might well have grave and even final reservations about performing such acts no matter how proportionally appropriate they seem. One's repugnance at taking advantage of a person's utter vulnerability to treat him in ways one regards as morally indecent may thus take precedence over one's hatred of that person and one's just desire for revenge. For one may find that one accepts, on the level of personal morality, something very like the United States Constitution's Eighth Amendment ban on "cruel and unusual punishment" or Kant's injunction that the punishment of a criminal must be "kept entirely free of any maltreatment that would make an abomination of the humanity residing in the person suffering it."[22] Thus one's retributive hatred, driven by moral outrage against an injustice suffered and by a desire to make sure the perpetrator of the outrage gets his just deserts, may be doomed by one's own better nature to go forever unfulfilled – in spite of adequate opportunity for accurate fulfillment – because one's inherent moral decency blocks the steps necessary to attain perfect retribution. Thus the moral person may settle for less than perfect retribution or for no retribution at all.[23]

22 Immanuel Kant, *The Metaphysical Elements of Justice*, trans. John Ladd (Indianapolis: Bobbs-Merrill, 1965), p. 102. See also pp. 131-3. I have explored Kant's theory and the constitutional ban on cruel and unusual punishments in my "Cruel and Unusual Punishments," in *Retribution, Justice, and Therapy*. A slightly revised version of this appears at the close of Chapter 3 (pp. 138-57) in Jeffrie G. Murphy and Jules L. Coleman, *The Philosophy of Law: An Introduction to Jurisprudence* (Totowa, N.J.: Rowman & Allanheld, 1984).
23 "When the burden of revenge is assigned to lawful authority, victims still have the psychic satisfaction of seeing their assailants' punishment, but society is protected from the violent passions of unchecked avengers and *avengers themselves are protected from a weight that frequently proves too great for the more gentle side of human nature.*" Susan Jacoby, *Wild Justice: The Evolution of Revenge* (New York: Harper &

This concludes my case against hatred. Since I regard retributive hatred as in principle the natural, fitting, and proper response to certain instances of wrongdoing, I do not regard the passion itself as either immoral or irrational. (It is not the moral equivalent of a phobia.) I do, however, believe that it is generally both irrational and immoral to be *led*, to use Spinoza's phrase, by this dangerous and often blind passion. I have called the case against hatred a set of cautions; taken together these cautions constitute a body of reasons so profound that instances where it is acceptable to proceed in spite of them are, in my judgment, rare. Thus rational and moral beings would, I think, want not a world utterly free of retributive hatred but one where this passion is *both* respected *and* seen as dangerous, as in great need of reflective restraint.

Adam Smith, admiring retributive hatred when "graceful and agreeable" but realizing that this passion "must be brought down to a pitch much lower than that to which undisciplined nature would raise [it]," eloquently puts his balanced and measured case for the passion in words on which I could not improve:

> How many things are requisite to render the gratification of resentment completely agreeable, and to make the spectator thoroughly sympathize with our revenge? The provocation must first of all be such that we should become contemptible, and be exposed to perpetual insults, if we did not, in some measure,resent it. Smaller offenses are always better neglected; nor is there any thing more despicable than that forward and captious humor which takes fire upon every slight occasion of quarrel. We should resent more from a sense of the propriety of resentment, from a sense that mankind expect and require it of us, than because we feel in ourselves the furies of that disagreeable passion. There is no passion, of which the human mind is capable, concerning whose justness we ought to be so doubtful, concerning whose indulgence we ought so carefully to consult our natural sense of propriety, or so dili-

Row, 1983), p. 43, emphasis added. Jacoby's book is a fascinating study of revenge in literature, religion, and law.

gently to consider what will be the sentiments of the cool and impartial spectator. Magnanimity, or a regard to maintain our own rank and dignity in society, is the only motive which can ennoble the expressions of this disagreeable passion. This motive must characterize our whole style and deportment. These must be plain, open, and direct; free from petulance and low scurrility, but generous, candid, and full of all proper regards, even for the person who has offended us. It must appear, in short, from our whole manner, without our laboring affectedly to express it, that passion has not extinguished our humanity; and that if we yield to the dictates of revenge, it is with reluctance, from necessity, and in consequence of great and repeated provocations. When resentment is guarded and qualified in this manner, it may be admitted to be even generous and noble.[24]

24 Adam Smith, *The Theory of Moral Sentiments* (1759; Indianapolis: Liberty Press, 1982), p. 38. Smith speaks of resentment; but, since he views this passion as involving a desire for revenge, it is closer to what I have called retributive hatred. Since Smith gives a central place to concerns about rank and status, this might prompt some to dismiss his account of justified resentment as simply bourgeois prejudice. This, I think, would be a mistake. The status in question may be viewed as moral status (and thus a clear object of legitimate concern), and such status, since we are social creatures, may in large part depend on how others treat and regard us – may depend on what John Rawls calls the social dimension of self-respect. We should not, in short, trivialize all status worries by assuming that they all must be on a par with, for example, such inane concerns as where one is to be seated at a formal dinner.
    Of course, some (e.g., Socrates and Jesus) may claim that they derive their entire sense of their worth from non-social factors – in Jesus' case that He was the Son of God and for Christians, perhaps, that they are created in God's image and that their true and ultimate worth – their destiny – is to be found in the hereafter. Such persons could then reject utterly the social status dimension of moral worth that I find present in such writers as Aristotle, Smith, Hume, and Rawls. There might, however, be a price for such rejection . For example: Could this degree of insulation from others be compatible with true love or friendship or with meaningful membership in any human relationship or community? Recall Jesus' remark to his mother (John 2:4): "Woman, what have I to do with thee?"
    Sentiments similar to Smith's were earlier expressed by Aristotle – another thinker who is not overquick to express total condemnation of any natural human passion: "The person who is angry at the right things and towards the right people, and also in the right way, at the

right time, and for the right length of time, is praised. . . . The deficiency – a sort of inirascibility or whatever it is – is blamed, since people who are not angered by the right things, or in the right way, or at the right times, or towards the right people, all seem to be foolish. For such a person seems to be insensible and to feel no pain. Since he is not angered, he does not seem to be the sort to defend himself; and such willingness to accept insults to oneself and to overlook insults to one's family and friends is slavish" (*Nicomachean Ethics*, 1125b ff., trans. Terence Irwin [Indianapolis: Hackett, 1985]).

As both Smith and Aristotle make clear, it is not mandatory (only permissible) to inflict the hurt that will constitute the proper revenge. They also make clear that the hurt constituting the proper revenge must never exceed what is properly proportional to the injury and will often involve no more than the hurt feelings or shame that the wrongdoer will experience when righteous anger or public rebuke is directed toward him. Another important point they make is that a person who is large of spirit will try to pass off minor injuries and insults and will indulge himself in retributive hatred only rarely and as a last resort.

Chapter 4

The retributive idea

JEAN HAMPTON

"One day, a serf-boy, a little boy of eight, threw a stone in play and hurt the paw of the General's favourite hound. 'Why is my favourite dog lame?' He was told that the boy had thrown a stone at it and hurt his paw. 'Oh, so it's you, is it?' said the General looking him up and down. 'Take him!' They took him. They took him away from his mother, and he spent the night in the lock-up. Early next morning the General, in full dress, went out hunting. He mounted his horse, surrounded by his hangers-on, his whips, and his huntsmen, all mounted. His house-serfs were all mustered to teach them a lesson, and in front of them all stood the child's mother. The boy was brought out of the lock-up. It was a bleak, cold, misty autumn day, a perfect day for hunting. The General ordered the boy to be undressed. The little boy was stripped naked. He shivered, panic-stricken and not daring to utter a sound. 'Make him run!' ordered the General, 'Run, run!' the whips shouted at him. The boy ran. 'Sick him!' bawled the General, and set the whole pack of borzoi hounds on him. They hunted the child down before the eyes of his mother, and the hounds tore him to pieces. . . . Well, what was one to do with [the General]? . . . "
"Shoot him!" Alyosha said softly.
Fyodor Dostoevsky, The Brothers Karamazov

Jeffrie Murphy's qualified defense of retributive hatred prompts me to reconsider my categorization of the "hateful"

111

emotions. I argued in Chapter 2 that there is more than one variety of hatred, two of which – spiteful and malicious hatred – I contended were self-defeating, and another of which – moral hatred – I defended. Murphy suggests, in response, that there is a variety of hatred that I missed: like moral hatred this con-attitude involves opposition to a wrongdoer and his cause on moral grounds, but like malicious or spiteful hatred, it involves the desire either to hurt the wrongdoer or to see him suffer. Murphy names this emotion "retributive hatred." Is it true, as Murphy claims, that this is a distinctive and legitimate (albeit somewhat dangerous) form of hatred?

I. PROBLEMS WITH RETRIBUTION

For some readers, the existence of this emotion as a distinct and morally acceptable response to wrongdoing will seem obvious. Other readers, however, will be troubled by and suspicious of it: is there a justifiable reason, they wonder, why a victim who purportedly experiences such hate wants to see the wrongdoer suffer?

In Chapter 2 I offered explanations of why haters desire suffering for those they hate. Malicious and spiteful haters desire the suffering either to effect or to vindicate their sense of what their relative standings on a competitive ranking ladder should be. And any attempt by the moral hater to inflict pain on the one he hates is a means of securing victory over the hated one and his immoral cause. But if Murphy is right that there is a retributive hatred that is distinct from both of these responses, then neither of these reasons explains the appeal of the hated one's suffering for the person experiencing this emotion.

Murphy proposes both to explain and to justify this appeal by attributing to retributive haters the desire to see the hated one suffer for retributive reasons. But what are these reasons? Advocates of retribution typically answer that there is no *telos*, or goal, behind the suffering retributivists want: it is simply desired because it is supposed to be "fitting" or

112

"suitable" or "right." And in response to queries about *why* suffering is suitable for wrongdoers, retributivists typically insist that this question has no answer. It is supposed to be bedrock intuition that, at the very least, those who are not guilty ought not to suffer pain, and more positively, that those who are guilty deserve to suffer in proportion to the pain they have caused. J. L. Mackie claims that such ideas have for us an "immediate, underived moral appeal or moral authority."[1] And like Kant and Hegel, Mackie contends that "if we did not feel that there was such a positive retributivist reason for imposing a penalty, we should not feel that even sound arguments in terms of deterrence or reformation or any similar future benefit would make it morally right to inflict suffering or deprivation on the criminal."[2]

Those suspicious of retribution are generally unpersuaded by this kind of defense. Presumably they are the people who either do not find this firm "bedrock intuition" inside themselves or are suspicious of its authority and thus cannot be convinced by an unanalyzed appeal to it.[3] Accordingly, some retributivists have attempted to make sense of the supposed fittingness of inflicting suffering on a wrongdoer, with dubious results. For example, Nozick proposes that the punishment represents a kind of "linkage" between the criminal and "right values."[4] But why is inflicting pain on someone a way of effecting this linkage? Why isn't the infliction of a pleasurable experience for the sake of the crime just as good a way of linking the wrongdoer with these right values? If Nozick explains the linkage of pain with crime by saying that the pain is necessary to convey to the criminal that his actions

1 J. L. Mackie, "Morality and the Retributive Emotions," *Criminal Justice Ethics*, (1982), pp. 3–9.
2 Ibid., p. 4.
3 Mackie himself admits that there does not seem to be any readily understandable way of making sense of this idea and, as I will discuss later, proposes an evolutionary – and merely explanatory – derivation of retribution as a sentiment. See pp. 3–4.
4 Robert Nozick, *Philosophical Explanations* (Cambridge, Mass.: Harvard University Press, 1981), p. 374.

were wrong, then he has answered the question but lost his retributive theory, putting forward instead a variation of the theory justifying punishment as moral education.[5] Other philosophers, such as Hegel, speak of punishment as a way of annulling or cancelling the crime, and hence "deserved" for that reason.[6] But although these words have a nice metaphorical ring to them, it is hard to see how they can be given a literal force that will explain the retributivist's concept of desert. As Mackie notes, punishment cannot eliminate crimes in any literal sense, because future events never cause past events not to have happened.[7]

A different defense of retribution has been advocated by Herbert Morris, and although attracted to it in earlier writings, Murphy has recently come to question it.[8] On this view, retribution is characterized in terms of *distributive justice*. Laws are understood as constraints on behavior which society finds collectively beneficial; individuals who break those laws for individually rational reasons are subverting the system for private gain in a way that makes them similar to free riders (i.e., people who derive gain from a collective good without paying for that good). Punishment of these free riders is a way to "even up the score": the legal system takes away, by means of pain, the benefit these individuals derived from their lawbreaking.

5 See Herbert Morris, "The Paternalistic Theory of Punishment," in *Punishment and Rehabilitation*, ed. J. Murphy (Belmont, Calif.: Wadsworth, 1985); and Jean Hampton, "The Moral Education Theory of Punishment," *Philosophy and Public Affairs*, Summer 1984, pp. 245–73.
6 See his *Philosophy of Right*, ed. T. M. Knox (Oxford: Oxford University Press, 1976).
7 See Mackie, p. 4. Both Mackie and Herbert Fingarette (the latter in "Punishment and Suffering," *Proceedings of the American Philosophical Association*, 1977) review a variety of retributivist arguments in defense of the idea that wrongdoers deserve to suffer, all of which appear to come up short. Each also makes a positive proposal of his own. I consider Mackie's later in this chapter and Fingarette's in note 20.
8 See Herbert Morris, "Persons and Punishment," in Murphy, *Punishment and Rehabilitation*. Murphy discusses this paper and his new worries about it in note 10 to Chapter 3.

But what is this benefit? If it is the monetary gain from the crime, then compensation of the victim would be sufficient to take away the wrongdoer's benefit. Yet the retributivist would desire punishment over and above any compensation provided by, say, a thief to her victim. And on this view it would make no sense to punish unsuccessful offenders.

So perhaps the criminal's benefit which the punishment is supposed to take away is the elevation of utility that comes from being able to break off the restraints of society and pursue one's own good. On this view, a thief must be punished even after she has been made to compensate her victim, in order to take from her the advantage that comes from the lawbreaking itself. One immediate problem with this position is that because all lawbreakers have benefited in the same way and (it seems) to the same extent by throwing off the restraints of law, the position seems to require that all lawbreakers receive the same punishment. To avoid this problem, an advocate of the position would have to develop a theory that explains how those who break gravely important laws derive more benefit from so doing that those who violate less serious laws, so that the former deserve more punishment than the latter.

Suppose for the sake of argument that such a theory could be developed.[9] While there are some crimes which this position, supplemented by such a theory, might be thought to suit, such as thefts, embezzlements and property crimes generally, other crimes make the position look uncomfortably strange – even repulsive. Consider the crime of rape. Are we to understand that the reason we punish rapists is that we believe they derived a benefit from being able to rape (which is greater than that gained by those who merely steal cars or speed on the highway) that we wish *we* could have but which we prevent ourselves from enjoying because we believe such conduct, when performed on a widespread basis, is collectively disadvantageous? Or consider murder: do we envy the

9 See George Sher, *Desert* (Princeton, N.J.: Princeton University Press, 1987), which tries to do this.

murderer his freedom to satisfy his desires through killing, and punish him merely because we seek to take from him the advantage of being unrestrained in pursuit of his murderous desires, where that restraint is one we would willingly throw off but for our recognition that retaining it is mutually advantageous? Such suggestions seem ridiculous. The idea that punishment is simply the taking away of the *advantages* which rapists or murderers have by virtue of being unrestrained presupposes that we accept that their actions (or the consequences of the actions) are, at least in certain circumstances, inherently desirable and rational, and that we object to them only because, if performed by everyone, they would be collectively harmful. Hence it is a theory presupposing a position on the nature of criminal law and criminal acts which is (to use a phrase of Murphy's) too "creepy" to be right.[10]

But perhaps we can make it less creepy.[11] Suppose we say, not that the criminal gets an advantage from his crime, but that when he commits a crime he isn't paying the *cost* we are paying when we obey the law. Again, this makes him, in a different way, a free rider, because he enjoys the benefits of our cost paying while not paying them himself. But once again, although this theory may explain, in part, the nature of our condemnation of those who violate various sorts of property or tax laws, it does a poor job of accounting for condemnation of those who violate persons. If I refrain from murdering you, am I really imposing a cost on myself for the sake of creating a collectively advantageous social order? If I become angry at you for murdering, is my anger solely or even primarily about the fact that you haven't paid the cost I've paid but enjoyed the fact that I and others have paid it? Once again, such a view seems incorrect.

But the fact that it is incorrect teaches us something important: this theory of retribution fails in a fully adequate way to

10 J. Murphy, "The Justice of Economics," *Philosophical Topics*, 14 (Fall 1986), p. 206.
11 This more plausible line was suggested to me by Richard Gale.

link our condemnation of a wrongdoer *to that which makes his conduct wrong.*[12] The *right* theory of retribution is one that will be able to connect retributive punishment with the immorality of the conduct being punished.

Does Mackie's theory of retribution successfully link assessments of immorality with the retributive response? Mackie believes retribution is a *feeling* which has evolved in our species and which is much like the "bite back" response I briefly mentioned in Chapter 2. Even as dogs may bite and cats may scratch those who attack them, human beings, according to Mackie, feel the emotional urge to "hit" those who hurt them. Such "hitting" is unreasoned and unreasoning – it is instinctive in just the way that a snarl or a bite following a harm is instinctive in other mammals. So we snap at relatives, verbally spar with colleagues, and some of us even physically attack those who have hurt us. Mackie argues that this emotional response exists within us because it encourages cooperation among human beings by introducing a negative sanction for non-cooperation, so that it has been selected for and refined in our highly social species. Hence, this response is not something one engages in so that one might deter exploiters in the future; instead it is an instinct for attack following a harm engaged in for *no* reason, but which has been implanted in one as a member of the human species because of its deterring consequences. The instinct itself isn't teleological, but its existence in the human being is explained by the fact that it furthers this creature's efforts at survival.

Mackie found this style of explanation of retribution appealing insofar as it fits with advocates' defense of it as foundational while also making teleological sense of it. Appealing though it is, I would argue that this approach to retribution is at best incomplete. Mackie's theory implicitly denies to retribution any cognitive content. (Note that his

---

12 Except perhaps for property crimes. The free-rider explanation might provide at least part of the reason why these sorts of actions are immoral, accounting for the plausibility of the theory when it is applied to them.

referring to it as a 'sentiment' presupposes a non-cognitivist approach to the emotions, with which both Murphy and I disagree.) But cognitive content is precisely what those who defend retribution must understand the response to have if retribution is to *justify* the infliction of harm on wrongdoers. A primitive urge, which is all the bite-back response could be in other mammals, cannot by itself justify anything.[13] Mackie himself realizes this, and thereby justifies the harm his retributive sentiment calls for by appealing to the evolutionary advantages of the sentiment's existence in human beings; for Mackie *the sentiment itself* doesn't justify the harm. Yet traditional retributivists have insisted that retribution is an idea which does have justificatory force in and of itself: that wrongdoers deserve to suffer is supposed to be a good *reason* for inflicting harm on them.

Mackie's analysis also seems to provide us with too simple a characterization of the victim's state of mind. Consider Franny, the rape victim in John Irving's *The Hotel New Hampshire* (discussed by Murphy in note 7 to Chapter 3). Franny was an angry woman, and there might well have been something primitive and unreasoned about her anger. But she is also described as someone who, after satisfying her desire to harm the gang leader rapist, finally achieved *peace* by doing so. Now successful accomplishment of what instinct demands brings with it what we might call 'relief' (e.g., after sexual intercourse or a good meal), but 'peace' seems to describe a mental as well as a physical contentment. Franny badly *wanted* something which the harm to the gang leader could effect; once that harm was inflicted by her she got what she badly wanted, and this is the kind of situation in which people find themselves "at peace." Proponents of

---

13 Mackie himself believes this, and he argues that the retributive sentiment in human beings would have to be explained by making reference to its development in a social context. But he never explains how the sentiment's role in a society helps us to understand the sentiment in a more full-bodied way, or how it helps us to differentiate it from mere strike-back responses in more primitive creatures (some of whom, e.g., primates, are also social animals).

retribution would say Franny saw the suffering as "deserved," wanted it for that reason and achieved satisfaction and contentment after delivering it. But this notion of "desert" seems to be a cognitive element in Franny's emotional state. Mackie provides us with no explanation of what it is. So while I believe Mackie is probably right that there is a natural instinct for harming that frequently accompanies (although need not accompany) our attempts to inflict pain on those who wrong us, I would also argue that he is not correct to think that this is *all* retribution is. The concept of retributive desert has once again escaped analysis.

It is partly because retributivists have been at a loss to explain their notion of desert that I, along with others,[14] have proposed that retribution may be nothing more than revenge. Perhaps the retributivist's *lex talionis*, his "eye for an eye, tooth for a tooth" conception of punishment, is just a restatement of the kind of vengeance which victims frequently want. The wrongdoer inflicts one pain; the victim (or the society which represents him) reciprocates with a second. Aren't both parties simply engaged in a kind of competitive struggle for standing, in which harm is taken either to effect or to prove a diminishment of the other's position relative to one's own, a diminishment in which one glories?

Some of Murphy's examples encourage this dark thought. Consider his discussion of Ruth (in note 20 to Chapter 3) from Fay Weldon's novel *The Life and Loves of a She-Devil*, whose wish to get even with her former husband and his new wife drives her to extraordinary lengths until she successfully brings them low. Here is a woman whose demand for "justice" seems in fact to be a demand for a competitive victory over those she wants to diminish, and that is precisely the strategy of the malicious hater.

But Murphy describes other victims, whose interest in harming their assailants does not seem, at least at first

14 See my "Moral Education Theory of Punishment." And note that the Supreme Court justices' decision in *Furman v. Georgia* characterized retribution as "naked vengeance" arising from a need of our "baser selves" (408 U.S. 238, 1972: see pp. 304 and 345).

glance, spiteful or malicious. As discussed earlier, there is Franny, the character in Irving's *Hotel New Hampshire* who can achieve peace after suffering the trauma of gang rape only by causing harm to the gang's leader. And there are the real-life victims of the Camelback rapist; they vigorously campaigned for his receiving the maximum sentence allowed by law, outraged at the thought that his punishment should be anything short of severe, given what he had done to them. Murphy chides those who would criticize these women for such feelings, contending that, given what the rapist did to them, their demand that he suffer great pain is "natural, fitting, and proper."

Certainly we can sympathize with these women, and share their outrage at the rapist's deed. And we may experience the same sort of outrage if we dwell on personal experiences in which others have badly wronged us. But people who angrily insist on intense suffering for their wrongdoers do not strike us as *noble* or in any way exceptionally meritorious (in contrast, for example, to people who, like Jesus, "forgive from the cross"). Perhaps the only reason we are reluctant to criticize these victims for their hatred is because we believe they are already experiencing too much pain to make it right to inflict any more. Moreover, when Murphy describes what Franny wants when she experiences what he takes to be the retributive emotion, he uses the word 'revenge' (Chapter 3, note 7), suggesting once again that her emotion is in fact malicious hatred, which merits moral criticism.

Proponents of retribution maintain, in the face of such doubts, that there can be something profoundly ignoble, even despicable, about someone who would block or deny the retributivist response following at least *some* crimes. Consider the story told by Ivan to his brother Alyosha in *The Brothers Karamazov*, quoted at the beginning of this chapter. How could even the most loving Christian saint resist the thought that a man who would set dogs on an innocent child and force his mother to watch the boy being torn to pieces should die? Turning the other cheek towards such a monster seems villainous.

Does Christianity insist on such villainy? One might well think so if one notes the many passages in which Jesus is hostile to the *lex talionis*:

> You have learned that they were told, "Eye for eye, tooth for tooth." But what I tell you is this: Do not set yourself against the man who wrongs you. . . . You have heard that they were told "Love your neighbor, hate your enemy." But what I tell you is this: Love your enemy and pray for your persecutors: only so can you be children of your heavenly father, who makes the sun rise on the good and the bad alike, and sends the rain on the honest and dishonest. (Matt. 5:38–9, 43–5)

The sunshine and the rain are for us all because God loves us as his children. Surely, if we are to follow the Lord's example, we must not strive to hurt those who are his beloved children, and our own spiritual brothers and sisters, no matter what they do to us.

Yet this may be far too saccharine a portrait of Christianity's requirements, given other actions and teachings of Jesus. There is the famous incident in which he angrily overthrows the tables of the moneychangers in the temple of Jerusalem (Matt. 21:12–13); there are his ruthless judgements of the scribes and Pharisees: "Woe unto you, scribes and Pharisees, hypocrites! For ye are like unto white-washed sepulchres, which outwardly appear beautiful, but inwardly are full of dead men's bones; and of all uncleanness" (Matt. 23:27);[15] and there is his invocation of hell: "Ye serpents, ye offspring of vipers [said to the Pharisees], how shall ye escape the judgement of hell?" (Matt. 23: 33). Jesus sounds here like an angry Old Testament prophet, and doesn't that anger presuppose the judgement that these people are wicked and deserve to suffer, at least the fire of his words,

15 He also warns the people: "Beware of the scribes, who desire to walk in long robes, and to have salutations in the marketplaces, and chief seats in the synagogues, and chief places at feasts; they that devour widows' houses and for a pretence make long prayers; these shall receive greater condemnation" (Mark 12:38–40).

and maybe even the fires of hell? (See, e.g., Luke 13:1–5 or Matt. 5:29–30.)

How do we reconcile Jesus' retributive-sounding anger with his attacks on the *lex talionis*, his insistence on loving one's enemies and his encouragement of forgiveness? Perhaps we cannot. Perhaps Jesus' teachings are informed by the claims both of love and of justice, the latter prompting an anger which he cannot deny but which he is afraid to recommend or approve because it violates what love requires.

And perhaps Jesus' dilemma is also our dilemma: even though we value and encourage love towards our fellow human beings, prompting us to forgive them when they wrong us, we also seem to respect the idea that the guilty deserve to pay in pain for the wrongs they cause others, a thought generally encased in an anger that drives out love. There does not seem to be any easy way to reconcile these two responses to wrongdoing, nor is it easy to give either response up. Yet they coexist uneasily within us.

II. MAKING SENSE OF THE RETRIBUTIVE IDEA

The preceding section showed the problems one faces if one wants to endorse the idea of retribution. They are problems that I have decided to take on, insofar as examples of criminals such as Dostoevsky's General seem to make the retributive idea virtually irresistible. But to endorse retribution, I must satisfy myself that it makes sense as a legitimation of harm, and is importantly different from the vengefulness that emanates from malice. Even more ambitiously, I believe I must argue, *contra* Murphy, that *retribution is not a form of hatred at all*, so that (as Jesus may have been trying to say) the claims of love need not be violated by the claims of justice, or vice versa. This is not an easy task. As we have seen, the project of "making sense" of retribution in order to show how it is different from revenge has been attempted before and is notoriously difficult to pull off. Explanations of retribution either miss the mark entirely or else presuppose the very idea they try to explain, perhaps because, as Mackie says, people are "so firmly wedded to retributivist thinking that they find it difficult to confront the task of justifying retribution from cold, without implicitly assuming what they are setting out to explain."[16] Moreover, advocates of retribution who are convinced it is a bedrock intuition will believe I am foolish to try to analyze it; a foundational moral idea cannot be broken into pieces, nor can it be explained by something more fundamental.

I do not believe retribution is foundational. Instead I believe it gets its irresistible character by being the conjunction of two basic ideas mandating the harm of the wrongdoer as a means to an end. (I will not, as Murphy did, merely suppose that those who have the retributive sentiment desire to inflict retributive suffering on their wrongdoers; I will attempt to show two ways in which that retributive suffering is desirable.) Those who believe deeply that retribution is deontological may well object to my teleological reduction of it; as I noted earlier, retributivists have been loath to admit that retributive punishment has any goal in sight. But revenge itself seemed goalless before its strategic character was uncovered. So might there also be a hidden goal in a victim's call for retribution?

I will argue that there is. To put it metaphorically (but in a way that I hope is evocative), I will argue that those who want retribution want to inflict suffering that is taken to be the victim's value "striking back" and in this way proving itself. But why must a victim's value strike back by means of pain? And how does painful retaliation constitute vindication of the victim's worth? Just like Nozick, I must explain why pain effects a linkage between the criminal and what is true about a victim's value.

But before pursuing this idea, let me point out that because I will understand retribution as a communication about the wrongdoer's value, my analysis of it presupposes a theory of

16 Mackie, "Morality and the Retributive Emotions," p. 6.

human worth. As I said in Chapter 2, there are a variety of such theories, and what *kinds* of punishment a retributivist will recommend depends upon which theory she accepts (although the *point* of the retributive punishment will be the same, no matter what theory of human worth is presupposed).[17] For now, let me illustrate the theory using a Kantian theory of human worth, which makes people intrinsically, objectively and equally valuable. Aside from the fact that I believe this is the theory retribution ought to presuppose, I will also maintain that it is the theory its advocates generally do presuppose.

Retributive idea 1: punishment as a defeat. Those who wrong others, on the definition developed in Chapter 2, objectively demean them. They incorrectly believe or else fail to realize that others' value rules out the treatment their actions have accorded the others, and they incorrectly believe or implicitly assume that their own value is high enough to make this treatment permissible. So, implicit in their wrongdoings is a message about their value relative to that of their victims.

Now consider again a wrongdoer we discussed in Chapter 2, the neighborhood bully, whose *raison d'être* is to establish his superiority over those he beats up. A child who has been victimized by this bully and who desires in turn to beat him up may be neither spiteful nor malicious: rather than try to elevate himself by defeating the bully, he may simply want to establish that the bully is not elevated above him – or, indeed, above anyone. The child therefore aims to *defeat* the bully, and the defeat is supposed to be proof that the bully is not the "lord" he has claimed to be. I take this child to be characteristic of someone who desires retributive punishment.

Readers of Chapter 2 should recognize the child's action as

17 However, although I am not able to develop this idea here, I doubt that those who hold an instrumental theory of human worth can make use of it to ground any kind of retributive response.

an attempt at diminishment in the first sense defined there, that is, an attempt to diminish the wrongdoer's sense of his own value. Such diminishment was not itself taken to be a wrong in that chapter; it was only deemed a wrong if a wrongdoer's value was taken to preclude it so that it could be considered demeaning treatment. But the child's attempt at diminishment is aimed at conveying what the child takes to be the truth about how valuable the bully is relative to himself and to others. And I will argue that it is *not* demeaning to accord someone treatment designed to represent the *truth* about his value relative to others (assuming, of course, that it really does represent the truth).

However, the child is after more than diminishment in this sense. A retributivist's commitment to punishment is not merely a commitment to taking hubristic wrongdoers down a peg or two;[18] it is also a commitment to asserting moral truth in the face of its denial. If I have value equal to that of my assailant, then that must be made manifest after I have been victimized. By victimizing me, the wrongdoer has declared himself elevated with respect to me, acting as a superior who is permitted to use me for his purposes. A false moral claim has been made. Moral reality has been denied. The retributivist demands that the false claim be corrected. The lord must be humbled to show that he isn't the lord of the victim. If I cause the wrongdoer to suffer in proportion to my suffering at his hands, his elevation over me is denied, and moral reality is reaffirmed. I master the purported master, showing that he is my peer.

So I am proposing that retributive punishment is the defeat of the wrongdoer at the hands of the victim (either directly or indirectly through an agent of the victim's, e.g., the state) that symbolizes the correct relative value of wrongdoer and victim.[19] It is a symbol that is conceptually

18 Iakovos Vasiliou has suggested to me that it may be possible to link this analysis of retribution to the Greek concept of hubris.
19 In what follows, I speak of there being victims of crimes, but I do not point out the way in which every member of a society can be considered a victim of some sorts of wrongdoings (e.g. felonies). Were this

required to reaffirm a victim's equal worth in the face of a challenge to it. Thus the punishment has a *telos*, but the *telos* is not so much to produce good as it is to establish goodness.[20]

How does the infliction of pain constitute such a symbol? The answer is that pain conveys defeat – so that if defeat could be accomplished in some other way, presumably the child would be just as likely to use it as he would to use pain. But *any non-painful method*, so long as it was still a method for *defeating* the wrongdoer, *would still count as punishment*. Indeed, if one considers the wide variety of experiences which count as punishment in our society but which are not inherently painful (e.g., requiring public service), one realizes that what makes any experience the suffering of punishment is not the objective painfulness of the experience, but the fact that it is one the wrongdoer is *made* to suffer and one which represents his *submission* to the punisher. To use a phrase of Fingarette's, punishment is an experience designed to "humble the will" of the person who committed the wrongdoing.[21] And such humbling is generally disliked and found to be painful, perhaps explaining why punishment is so often confused with the infliction of pain. A better synonym for 'punishment,' according to Fingarette,[22] is the infliction of *suffering* (some meanings of 'suffer,' according to the *OED*, being "endure," "submit," "be subjected to") so that "in the respect that we suffer, we experience what we do not will, or in a stronger sense, we experience what is *against* our will." But I propose that the most general and accurate definition of 'punishment' is:

the experience of defeat at the hands of the victim (either directly or indirectly through a legal authority).

idea to be incorporated into the discussion, wrongdoers would have to "pay" not only for what they did to particular people but also for what they did to all of us.

20 I am indebted to Richard Gale for this way of putting things, and for pressing me about many of the ideas in this section.
21 See Fingarette, "Punishment and Suffering."
22 Ibid., p. 510.

If punishment is understood in this way, it appears morally problematic not only insofar as it may involve the infliction of pain but, more important, because it *always* involves the attempt to master another human being. I want to argue, however, that such mastery is morally wrong, that is, demeaning, *only* when it aims to establish something false about the relative value of the one claiming it (i.e., the one we call *wrong*) and of his victim; it is not morally wrong if the point of the mastery is to deny the wrongdoer's false claim to superiority and to assert the victim's equal value.[23]

But exactly how does punishment make this assertion? Consider that retributivists typically endorse the *lex talionis* as a punishment formula, or (as I would reinterpret it) as a formula for determining the extent to which the wrongdoer must be mastered. That formula calls for a wrongdoer to suffer something like what his victim suffered, and as Murphy notes, it is frequently mocked by those who point out that delivering to the criminal what he delivered to the victim can

---

23 This defense of retribution sounds, in some respects, like Fingarette's, but it is worthwhile pointing out the difference between the two accounts. Like Fingarette, I see punishment as the experience of submission, of being dominated. But Fingarette justifies punishment *only* by a legal institution. And the point of its infliction is to make the wrongdoer recognize that he is required not to defy the law's imperatives, that is, in order to see that the law (and not he himself) is "boss." This justification of retribution succeeds only as long as the law is a legitimate institution, and Fingarette offers no such justification for it. He also offers no justification of the punishment practices of non-legal institutions such as schools and families. So at best his is only a partial explanation of retributive thinking, that is, such thinking in legal contexts. Moreover, Fingarette's account is a strikingly non-moral explanation of the retributive idea, one which he believes is necessary if the law is not to be confused with morality. But surely retributivists such as Kant have taken retribution to be a deeply moral notion – perhaps even part of the bedrock of moral thought. To offer a non-moral explanation of it seems, therefore, to misrepresent the idea fundamentally. I am inclined to think his account might be right as part of the reason a legal system punishes, but wrong as an account of retribution. My account of retribution tries to explain its moral core, a core which I believe a variety of institutions, including the law as well as families and universities, make use of in pursuing both moral and non-moral objectives.

be impossible or ridiculous or both in many instances. But the punishment formula does not seem quite so silly if it is interpreted as calling *only* for proportionality between crime and punishment. To inflict on a wrongdoer something comparable to what he inflicted on the victim is to master him in the way that he mastered the victim. The score is even. Whatever mastery he can claim, she can also claim. If her victimization is taken as evidence of her inferiority relative to the wrongdoer, then his defeat at her hands negates that evidence. Hence the *lex talionis* calls for a wrongdoer to be subjugated in a way that symbolizes his being the victim's equal. The punishment is a second act of mastery that denies the lordship asserted in the first act of mastery.

A critic might query this analysis by worrying that even if retributive punishment is one way to achieve this end, it might not be the only way or even the best way. And if there is another way to reassert the victim's value that is as good as, or better than, the punitive method, then why shouldn't the retributivist permit or prefer that method, and suspend the punishment of the wrongdoer – something a "hardcore" retributivist would presumably never want to do?

But I contend that punishment is uniquely suited to the vindication of the victim's relative worth, so that no other method purporting to achieve vindication could be preferred to it.[24] Suppose we gave a victim a ticker-tape parade after the crime to express our commitment to his value. Still the fact that he had been mastered by the wrongdoer would stand. He would have lost to her, and no matter how much the community might contend that he was not her inferior, the loss counts as evidence that he is. Hence *the victim wants*

24 But consider the fact that Martin Luther King, Jr., is acknowledged as the great champion of the rights (and thus the value) of blacks, and yet he never inflicted punishment. Strategies such as civil disobedience might be almost as effective (maybe even as effective), in certain circumstances, as punitive defenses of worth. Still, one wonders whether King and others chose their non-violent method of fighting criminality because the superior, punitive method was denied them.

the evidence nullified.[25] And punishment is the best way to do that. The wrongdoer can't take her crime to have established or to have revealed her superiority if the victim is able to do to her what she did to him. The punishment is therefore a second act of mastery that negates the evidence of superiority implicit in the wrongdoer's original act.

What is the retributivist's motive for wanting to reaffirm the equal worth of wrongdoer and victim?

His retributive motive should not be confused with a variety of non-retributive motives he might have. For example, he might see the communication as having desirable deterring effects both for the criminal and for the larger society. Or he may believe that it can morally educate the criminal and the society, on the grounds that the wrongdoer's loss to his victim (or to that victim's societal representative) will force both parties to reassess their relative value.[26] He may also desire to inflict punishment in order to benefit the victim,

25 The evidence is neither made to vanish by punishment nor made never to have existed. Instead it is explained away. Copernicus didn't make the evidence of the sun's literally rising vanish, but he did nullify it in the sense that he showed it wasn't really evidence for that conclusion. Similarly, punishment undercuts the probative force of the evidence of his superiority provided by the wrongdoer's action. I am indebted to Richard Healey for helping me to clarify this point.

26 Non-malicious victors will wish wrongdoers to conclude not that "this victim (or his government representative) is now my superior because he can force me to submit to his will" but, rather, that "I am not more valuable than anyone else, and my loss to this person is a sign of that fact" or, as children generally put it, that "I'm not better than anyone else." Moreover, if the wrongdoer is defeated because he hurt you, then he is aware of a cost to future transgressions that will make him (and others) less likely to commit them in the future. He is also aware that the *fact* that you have a protective response makes you someone he has to "take into account" in his calculations about how to achieve his goals. You aren't a "nobody" he can "walk all over." This is not to say that the punishment will make him respect you in the right way, to the extent that you deserve. But it may well make him "fear" you to some extent, and for a person seeking some acknowledgement of her worth, this is at least a start. As I argue in "The Moral Education Theory of Punishment," it may have more sophisticated educative effects on the criminal.

who may feel a resentment or hatred that is fed by a fear that the crime has revealed her as or made her lower. (A major reason why Franny was so pleased at being able to harm the gang leader may be that the harming confirmed in her own mind that those who raped her were not her superiors.) Perhaps some of the impatience felt by victims towards people, such as myself, who have advocated punishment as a way of morally educating criminals stems from the fact that we have tended to see the suffering as helpful only to the one who did the harming or to society members tempted to do what he did, and thus have ignored the very real help to the victim's injured self-esteem which she can and should get from the defeat of her assailant.

But the *retributive* motive for inflicting suffering is to annul or counter the appearance of the wrongdoer's superiority and thus affirm the victim's real value.[27] So even in a situation where neither the wrongdoer nor society will either listen to or believe the message about the victim's worth which the "punitive defeat" is meant to carry, and where the victim doesn't need to hear (or will not believe) that message in order to allay any personal fears of diminishment, the retributivist will insist on the infliction of punishment insofar as it is a way of "striking a blow for morality" or (to use a phrase of C. S. Lewis's) a way to "plant the flag"[28] of morality. Recall that an adequate theory of retribution would show how it was a response to what was immoral about the wrongdoer's action. This is precisely what the present theory tries to do. If punishment symbolizes the reassertion of the victim's value, it is desired by one who is responding to and rejects the denial of that value by the criminal's action (where

---

27 So punishment is expressive. See Joel Feinberg, "The Expressive Function of Punishment," *Doing and Deserving* (Princeton, N.J.: Princeton University Press, 1970).

28 C. S. Lewis, *The Problem of Pain* (New York: Macmillan, 1944), p. 45. Quoted by Robert Nozick in his *Philosophical Explanations*, p. 718 n. 80. The complete passage is: "It plants the flag of truth within the citadel of a rebel soul." So expanded, it sounds a bit too educative to be a purely retributive sentiment.

that denial is what makes the action immoral). And one's commitment to that value can motivate one to carry out that reassertion even when one is quite sure that the defiance will persist despite the message.

This reassertion may be what Hegel meant when he spoke of the way punishment "annuls the crime." Of course it can't annul the act itself, but *it can annul the false evidence seemingly provided by the wrongdoing of the relative worth of the victim and the wrongdoer.* Or to put it another way, it can annul the message, sent by the crime, that they are not equal in value.

We might also use this approach to retribution to explain Kant's famous concern to punish criminals even when the society of which they are members is about to disband:

> Even if a civil society were to dissolve itself by common agreement of all its members (for example if the people inhabiting an island decided to separate and disperse themselves around the world), the last murderer remaining in prison must first be executed, so that everyone will duly receive what his actions are worth and so that the bloodguilt thereof will not be fixed on the people because they failed to insist on carrying out the punishment; for if they fail to do so, they may be regarded as accomplices in this public violation of legal justice.[29]

I agree with Kant that we would be accomplices in the crime if we failed to punish its perpetrator, because we would be condoning the evidence it gave us of the relative worth of victim and offender, or to put it another way, because we would be acquiescing in the message it sent about the victim's inferiority. Kant takes it as fundamental that to be committed to morality is to be committed to asserting and defending it no matter what the consequences. Hence it is morally required that we send an annulling message after a crime so that the victim's value receives its proper defense.

These last remarks should make it clear that this analysis of retribution presents it as something other than a justification of punishment designed to convey a moral lesson to the

29 Immanuel Kant, *The Metaphysical Elements of Justice*, trans. John Ladd (Indianapolis: Bobbs-Merrill, 1965), p. 102.

wrongdoer or to society. Indeed, it may be that *part of what it is to view an action as immoral is to have the desire to reassert the victim's value through punishment.*[30] But having made this proposal, I want to argue that such an assertion makes sense (and appears justifiable) only if people are at least able to understand the symbolic significance of the punishment, albeit perhaps unwilling to do so. Imagine Kant's island suddenly hit by toxic fumes which mentally disable all but one person; would that person still believe he would be the accomplice of the one responsible if he desisted from punishing her? Wouldn't the punishment of an individual who can neither remember the crime nor understand what the punishment is about, in a community of people who are no better able than she to comprehend either, seem a meaningless cruelty? My point is that even if retributivists insist that their main reason for reasserting value through punishment is not to effect moral education but to utter moral truth whether or not anyone bothers to listen, in fact one would bother to utter it only in a world where the truth can be comprehended. So the retributivist is concerned with 'education' in an attenuated sense of the word insofar as he wants the moral truth to be heard, but is not intent on successful persuasion or criminal reform; he wants to annul the criminal's message and reassert the moral truth, but does not perceive punishment as a certain cure for immorality.

We have set the stage for another question: should one punish a wrongdoer who is unable to understand the assertion behind the punishment even if the rest of society is able to comprehend it? This question has contemporary relevance to those disturbed by some people's enthusiasm for the punishment of Nazi war criminals who are now senile, and who ramble and drool through their trials. Here too I think a retributivist who appreciates what retributive punishment is for would refrain from inflicting it. Such punishment is sup-

---

30 Perhaps the conceptual linkage between the judgement of an action as immoral and its punishment exists only if there is a certain kind of practice or conception of morality in society.

posed to be a defeat; but if a wrongdoer has changed so that he has lost considerable rationality and now cannot understand that he is defeated or why that defeat has occurred, then the man who was able to, and who did, defy the facts of others' value no longer exists. Now it was that agent who implicitly claimed superiority over the victim through his action. He is therefore the one who must be defeated. But he is gone, and in his place is an individual whose value as a human being without agency may be problematic to assess. The time for punishment is passed, just as surely as if the wrongdoer had died.

Do these remarks raise problems for the retributive punishment of reformed criminals? No; one would think so only if one mistook retributive punishment for moral education. But retribution isn't about making a criminal better; it is about denying a false claim of relative value. The reformed and penitent murderer (who retains the capacity to understand what he has done) is still (for moral purposes) the same person who committed the murder, because he retains the agency which produced the murder (i.e., he is still an agent who chose to perform this act). Thus he is the one who implicitly claimed superiority over the victim through the crime, and he remains the one who must be levelled in order to negate the evidence of superiority provided by the crime. If he is truly penitent, he may be just as interested in seeing that claim denied as the family of the victim. It is not uncommon for remorseful wrongdoers to seek out punishment, seeing it as a way of making up for what they did to their victims. On my theory, "making it up to them" means, "voluntarily undergoing an experience which symbolizes that one is *not* as great in value, relative to them, as one's wrongdoing made it appear." (This is not to say that there are no problems surrounding the retributive punishment of reformed wrongdoers, as I shall discuss in the final section of this chapter.)

Let us return to the retributivist's punishment formula. As I said, the retributivist's endorsement of the *lex talionis* is the insistence on proportionality between crime and punishment. The more severe the offense, the more severe the punishment is supposed to be. But this makes sense if punishment is a defeat for the wrongdoer in the name of the victim which is intended to express the victim's value. The more severe the punishment, the more he is being brought low; and how low we want to bring a criminal depends on the extent to which his actions symbolize his superiority and lordship over the one he hurt. The higher wrongdoers believe themselves to be (and thus the more grievously they wrong others), the harder and farther they must fall if the moral reality of the parties' relative value is to be properly represented. So the increasing harshness of punishment symbolizes the increasing severity of the violation of the valuable entity. The value will "strike back" more severely against more severe transgressions of it.

Thus if the Camelback rapist, who used his victims for his own satisfaction as if they were his slaves, were to receive a light sentence, this would be a small defeat for him. What he has done to them turns out to be vastly more than what they are able (either directly or through their legal representatives) to do to him, a fact that seems to symbolize his persistent superiority over them despite his having been sentenced. So he has gotten away with something: he has gotten away with a claim of relative superiority. Society has failed to annul that claim successfully. And the fact that it is not annulled can brutalize the rapist's victim more thoroughly than his original attacks did.

Of course, it "brutalizes" them only if one takes it that they are right to claim they are his equals. Sexist or racist or caste-based societies might insist that some victims are not the equals of their assailants, so that the assault is either not wrong in the first place (for example, a slave owner in the American South could not be understood to have raped any of his slaves) or not as wrong as the victim might try to argue (a society might contend that the wife beater deserves a mild rebuke, but not a jail term). On the other hand, such a society would view an inferior's assault of a superior as worse than the latter's assault of the former, so that the inferior's assault should receive punishment that causes more suffering than the crime committed, not only to counter the evidence of the wrongdoer's relative superiority, but also to provide evidence of his relative inferiority. So to the extent that a retributivist does not hold an egalitarian theory of human worth, he will not endorse the *lex talionis* as the appropriate punishment formula. How much a wrongdoer must be defeated depends on what one believes the relative worth of victim and offender to be. Still, it is interesting that retribution is normally identified with the *lex talionis*, showing, I think, how thoroughly infected that theory of punishment is with an egalitarian theory of our value.

Our discussion of the retributivist's formula is still not complete: a good retributivist generally wants limits placed on punishment sentences. Moreover, the retributivist would prefer that these limits come not from *outside* his theory (so that without modification by external moral considerations the theory would be taken to endorse, say, torturing torturers) but from *within* the theory (so that the theory itself has the resources to rule out torture, no matter what the wrongdoer has done). Retributivists have, however, generally despaired of being able to do this. They have instead tended to devise what seems to be morally required external criteria for drawing the line between permissible and impermissible punishment. Thus Murphy speaks in Chapter 3 of "intrinsically immoral" actions which one's "inherent moral decency" won't permit one to perform as punishments, and he uses the Constitution's phrase 'cruel and unusual' to try to pick out those punishments which are prohibited. But these phrases are not precise either in picking out or in explaining what counts as illicit treatment.

I want to propose that we might be able to set the limits of retributive punishment by using the internal resources of the theory as I have interpreted it, assuming a Kantian theory of human worth. Consider that on my analysis, genuinely non-malicious retributivists have as the aim behind the infliction of suffering not the vengeful diminishment of the criminal to a bestial level but the vindication of the victim's value. This

aim means that the punisher must not do anything that could
be interpreted as an attempt not merely to deny wrongdoers'
claim to superiority but also to *degrade* them, that is, cause
them in some way to lose value. Sometimes a crime is ghastly
in the way it portrays the victim as vastly lower than the criminal or in the way it seems to reduce him almost to a bestial
level, for example, mutilation, torture, enslavement. The *lex
talionis* would license doing the same thing to the wrongdoer
as a way of making the equal status of the victim manifest.
But to one who is committed to the idea that the wrongdoer
has an intrinsic value that is equal to the value of others, such
treatment can be hard, if not impossible, to stomach. One
cannot see the punishment as reasserting the moral facts if it
involves doing something to the wrongdoer that either
makes him or represents him to be degraded below the level
of human beings generally. Of course, the next question to be
asked is, Why isn't *every* punishment in violation of those
facts insofar as it is an attempt to master a human being
whose value is supposed to be intrinsic, permanent (for as
long as he remains a human being) and equal to that of others? Retributivists can reply that there are methods of mastery that deny the criminal's claim to lordship and that may
be severe if the criminal has gravely mistreated his victim,
but which are nonetheless not so harsh that they are identical
either to the treatments which are considered permissible
only for entities far less valuable than human beings or to
treatments which actually make them less valuable. Being
made to pay a fine or perform a public service or suffer con-
finement (under humane conditions) is to experience subju-
gation and defeat, but (at least arguably) none of these is
appropriate only for something subhuman, nor do they
make one subhuman. On the other hand, having an eye
gouged out, having acid thrown in one's face, losing fingers,
being tortured – these are treatments one would refuse to
consider permissible for animals, much less humans, and
which may damage people so as to cause them (at least to
appear) to lose value. So the retributivist who is committed
to reasserting moral truth must beware that her way of reas-

serting it does not implicitly deny for the criminal what it seeks to establish for the victim. Or alternatively, if the retributivist wants to establish the relative equality of victim and offender, he does not want to treat the offender in such a way that her value as a human being is denied. (So I would argue that one reason why capital punishment is controversial is that it is simply not clear whether execution does deny value.)

The *lex talionis* therefore cannot, by itself, be the appropriate punishment formula for the sophisticated retributivist, because there is no upper limit to the amount of pain it would require a wrongdoer to suffer for his crime, other than "what he did to his victim" – a limit that could well be far too high. A more accurate retributivist formula would call for comparability of punishments with crimes within certain limits that reflect the value of the wrongdoer, and a policy towards constructing punishments that would give the best expression possible of the value of the person hurt by the wrongdoer subject to these limits. To strike a blow for morality and thus for the idea that all human beings have great value, the victim must make sure that she fights in a way that recognizes the wrongdoer's very real value; she must, to use Kant's phrase, defeat him in such a way that she continues to "respect humanity in his person."

If this analysis of retribution is right, we can understand why retribution and revenge are importantly different, but nonetheless easily confused. The vengeful hater does not respect but aims to diminish the worth of the offender (either by representing it as lower or by making it lower) in order to elevate herself, a strategy that I have argued is self-defeating. The retributivist, on the other hand, aims to defeat the wrongdoer in order to annul the evidence provided by the crime of his relative superiority. The retributivist is interested in asserting moral truth; hence he is always mindful of, and respectful towards, the value of his wrongdoer. Indeed, the retributivist who accepts an egalitarian theory of worth has *no* interest in doing anything to *change* the value of either the wrongdoer or the victim. Instead, he is interested in using his domination to deny the wrongdoer's prior claim of superiority. Although he is like some avengers, namely, those who want to reveal wrongdoers to be lower than the crime makes them appear, nonetheless, he wants them diminished to a level that is correct and equal to the level of their victims. Nor is there anything self-defeating about his project: he is not using a competitive victory to elevate the victim; instead, he is using the victory to symbolize the equality in value and rank of victim and wrongdoer. Even a retributivist who accepts a hierarchical theory of human worth is uninterested in winning over the wrongdoer in order to elevate the victim. Instead he wishes to master the criminal so as to deny her prior claim to a higher place in the hierarchy, relative to the victim, than she in fact occupies. Again, there is nothing self-defeating about the retributivist's goal: he is using a competitive victory to deny an incorrect claim about relative rank.

But having isolated the difference between retribution and revenge, we can appreciate how close the two responses are (so that many victims may slide, unaware, back and forth between them). Both responses involve the desire to inflict pain as a way of mastering another, and both see such mastery as making a point about the relative value of offender and victim. But the point each wants to make is different. The vengeful hater masters the offender either to make the offender low in rank in order to elevate herself or to reveal the offender as low in rank and thereby reveal herself as higher, where the mastery is supposed to be competitive proof of superiority. Alas, this elevation is actually defeated rather than achieved by her diminishment of the offender. The retributivist, on the other hand, wants incorrect evidence of superiority denied and the victim's value reaffirmed. The punitive mastery of the wrongdoer is perceived not as a competitive victory that elevates the victim but, rather, as a denial of the wrongdoer's claim to elevation over (or relative to) the victim.

Retributive idea 2: punishment as vindicating value through protection. The preceding argument was an attempt to explain a way in which the wrongdoer could be "linked up with right values," and his crime "annulled," by inflicting punishment on him. The key idea in that argument was that punishment was the experience of defeat, designed to humble the wrong-doer and thus express his real worth relative to the victim. However, there is another way to make the connection between right values and pain. This connection can be made only when, for various reasons, *society* rather than the victim is responsible for carrying out punishment of wrongdoers.

No matter how else punishment is justified, its role as a deterrent is a primary reason why societies inflict it on criminals. The way it works to deter crime is not dissimilar to the way nature affords protection to many plants and animals. Consider the lowly nettle. To the naked eye, this plant has no obvious protection against damage. There are no visible thorns, it grows in readily accessible places rather than only on hard-to-reach crags or in deep ravines, and it is ubiquitous in summer. Yet anyone who touches it once is loath to do so again, because a chemical secretion from fine hairs on the leaves reacts with human skin to produce a prickly, burning sensation for several minutes. The nettle therefore enjoys a protective defense against human beings. It is a protection that does not stop someone from touching or damaging it (in the way that being encased in impenetrable glass would do); instead it is a protection that "strikes back" after human interference with the plant, thereby deterring future interference.

Punishment is analogous to a nettle's sting. The threat of suffering punishment is like the nettle's protective chemical secretion: a transgression activates an unpleasant experience such that future transgressions are deterred. Human beings, as I have already discussed, have an instinctive bite-back response which (as Mackie notes) may have evolved in us because of its desirable deterrent consequences. But reason as well as instinct directs us to harm wrongdoers in order to deter future crimes.

As retributivists are fond of pointing out, this can't be the whole story behind punishment, because victims see the punishment not only as a protection against the future but also as an appropriate response to the past, one that is *deserved* because of what was done. I now want to propose a second source of the retributivist's notion of desert, one that is *derived from* punishment's role as a deterrent but is quite different from deterrence.

Why should human beings have any kind of protection from attack, provided either by legal machinery or through social censure or ostracism? Clearly each of us has some ability to react against a transgressor, and some of us enjoy significant abilities in this area. But others of us, for instance, the newborn, the aged, the sick or the just plain weak, do not. One way to understand our practices of punishment is to see them as a societal attempt to deliver for each victim a protective "sting" against a transgressor which he may be ill-prepared or unable to deliver for himself.

But why should society want to afford each of us this protection? The answer to this question depends upon what theory of human worth one holds. One may believe that our worth derives from our ability to be of use to our fellows, so that society ought to protect each of us to the extent that we are instrumentally valuable to it. Or one may believe with Kant that human beings enjoy an equal and intrinsic worth, so that society should protect us equally. But whatever one's theory of human worth is, I am suggesting that societal punishment practices should be seen as created and designed to protect it. If society knew how to encase those it values in a substance that would protect them from all damage, it would surely do so (assuming it could afford to do so). But since no such protection is possible, it protects us in the way nettles are protected – by means of a kind of sting that is felt after a transgression and is intended to deter future transgressions.

Societies also have limited resources. How should they use these resources to punish wrongdoers? In particular, should all human beings be accorded the same protection? If there are some who are more valuable than most, shouldn't society protect them by a legally or socially created sting that is more severe than usual, and which is thus a better deterrent? And if there are people who are less valuable than others, shouldn't society protect them by a legally or socially created sting that is less severe than usual, thereby deterring less effectively? Not only are these grades of protection possible, but they exist in virtually every legal system that has ever been created, either officially or unofficially. I have already discussed the way in which racist, sexist or caste-based societies declare that some kinds of human beings are worth more than others; in these societies the punishment for those who injure the less valuable people is lighter than for those who injure the more valuable people. Statistics exist which support the view that killing a white man in the United States has historically been punished more severely than killing a black man.[31] Certain crimes against women by men in this and other societies have been lightly punished, and even condoned, for instance, rape or wife beating. One also sees differences in treatment in response to social status; the rich and powerful enjoy a more thorough and surer defense of their persons than do prostitutes, drug addicts and ghetto dwellers.

Accordingly, how society reacts to one's victimization can be seen by one as an indication of *how valuable* society takes one to be, which in turn can be viewed as an indication of how valuable one really is. This point is essential to understanding a societal component of the retributive idea. Of course a victim wants her assailant punished insofar as that punishment is one form of her defense against future crime. But she also wants her assailant punished by society in a way that is properly expressive of what she takes her value to be. *If legal punishment is a protection of one's value, then its infliction on a wrongdoer is a reflection of that value.* Because society's punishment protects those who are valuable, people who long for a high valuation may come to demand punishment, not only because they want this legal protection, but also

31 Hugo Bedau (ed.), *The Death Penalty in America*, 3rd ed. (Oxford: Oxford University Press, 1982); see the discussion of racial discrimination in the application of the death penalty in articles by Wolfgang and Reidel and by Bowers and Pace.

141

because they want the expression of what the legal protection symbolizes. (Witness a man who wants a high salary not only because he desires great wealth but also because he desires what great wealth in his profession symbolizes, e.g., career success, or great prowess on the job.)

Victims of criminals such as the Camelback rapist worry that if society allows the wrongdoer to suffer no painful consequences as a result of his action, he (and others) may conclude that the ones against whom he transgressed are not valuable enough for society to construct a significant protective barrier that exacts a (deterring) cost from one who would transgress it. So another idea behind victims' insistence that their wrongdoers shouldn't be allowed to "get away with it" is that society shouldn't allow the wrongdoers or the society to conclude, because of little or no protective response, that they were right to believe the victims lacked value relative to them. The rage felt by San Francisco's gay community after the light sentence given to Dan White, the murderer of Harvey Milk, was surely connected with their belief that the jury did not regard this homosexual as of sufficiently high value to punish his murderer severely. In their eyes the murderer *did* get away with something, namely, with the idea that as a white, male heterosexual he was of more value than Milk.[32]

So now we have two ways to link the infliction of suffering after a wrongdoing to the expression of the victim's worth. Both arguments attempt to capture and explain Nozick's intuition that retributive punishment is a way to link up a wrongdoer with right values and Hegel's idea that punishment in some sense "annuls" the crime. Earlier I expressed puzzlement over why *pain* was required to effect such a link-

---

32 But I do not endorse this reading of the light sentence. Given that Mayor Moscone (a heterosexual) was murdered along with Milk, the jury cannot be taken to have made a statement about homosexuals with its verdict, and its members were probably confused by a morally problematic California law on diminished capacity that obscured their good sense.

age or annul the crime. But as I said in discussing the first idea, punishment is not so much the infliction of pain as it is the infliction of a *defeat* that annuls the wrongdoer's claim of superiority, which such non-painful experiences as community service can deliver, just as well as pain (although because pain is commonly seen to represent defeat, it is a useful medium to symbolize the idea that the wrongdoer is not one's superior). And as I said in discussing the second idea, pain, or more generally, a humbling defeat which prideful wrongdoers will intensely dislike, can deter the commission of a crime against someone (or even something) having value; and the victim can come to see the value which the humbling defeat is meant to protect as symbolically expressed through the protection.

The Greeks talked of the Furies pursuing wrongdoers, torturing them for what they did. Each of us hopes that something like the Furies will doggedly pursue those who wrong us. Retributive punishment is our name for the Furies, and at a fundamental level it is punishment we desire because we see it, for the two reasons discussed in this section, as our *value* striking back at those who harmed us, and thus confirming that we *are* valuable, that their actions were indeed wrong and that we must be treated with respect.

III. WHAT IS RETRIBUTIVE HATRED?

Some readers may have already noted that if my analysis of retribution is right, it is not a species of hatred at all (although it can still qualify as part of a sentiment if sentiments are understood to have cognitive content). Someone who wants retribution may harbor neither love nor hate towards her wrongdoer. She is simply averse to the act and the message it carries, and desires to punish the wrongdoer in order to assert a different message implying that better treatment of the victim is required. Her attention is primarily on the crime, and on the victim's value; it is not on the criminal himself except insofar as his defeat is the way in which the communication of relative equality must be made.[33] Of course retribution may be accompanied by some form of aversion (perhaps quite considerable) towards the wrongdoer, but my point is that retribution itself carries no such opposition. The suffering is not meant as an expression of a con-attitude towards the criminal, but rather as a response that both offers protection for the victim and reasserts the victim's value. One reason why retribution might seem like such a good posture for a government to take as it punishes its criminals is that it is not a loving or a hateful posture (neither of which one might think a legal system ought to take).

But some readers (and Murphy himself) might find this remarkable! Surely victims who demand the suffering of their assailants, who call for the death penalty, who verbally attack their assailants in court, who bitterly recount what was done to them to all who will hear – surely these people hate their assailants. And I agree that they do. But this hatred is something other than a retributive response to the wrongdoer. It frequently accompanies retribution, but it is not the retributive response itself.

So what kind of hatred is it? Did we meet it in Chapter 2? Of course it might be the primitive, animal-like anger described earlier, which is unreasoned, has virtually no cognitive content and is experienced not only by human beings but by a wide variety of animals in response to an attack. But a human being's opposition to an assailant is generally more complicated than this. Unlike other animals, we can reflect upon those who have hurt us, and such reflection can generate different, more cognitively laden forms of anger.

It might also be the malicious or spiteful variants of hatred already discussed. In fact, I would argue that retribution is

33 This way of putting things makes one wonder why the retributive theory as I have outlined it doesn't make punishment of a criminal "a mere means to an end," so that he is being used when he is punished. The preceding section attempts to show that retributive punishment, properly understood, never involves acting towards the wrongdoer in such a way that his value is demeaned – which is what I would argue Kant *should* have meant by "treating someone as a mere means."

frequently accompanied by an unfortunate kind of malice. If we are resentful victims, determined to buttress our sense of our own value, we may desire to believe that the wrong-doer's act shows that she is worse than we are, measured on some kind of virtue scale which makes her our inferior. Thus we might call our assailant "trash" or an "animal" or a "Nazi." But readers of Chapter 2 should recognize the self-defeating strategy for securing elevation here, where value and rank are measured (at least in part) by one's level of virtue. Victims whose faces are twisted with rage as they clamor for harsh punishment of their assailants display all the ugliness of malicious hatred, so that however much we may sympathize with them, we still find them repulsive.

Moreover, I maintain that there are straightforward moral arguments against a spiteful or malicious response to a wrongdoing. In Chapter 2 I never argued that such responses were immoral, only that they were imprudent because self-defeating. But on what would moral injunctions against them be based? If something like Kant's theory of human worth is right, one reason for condemning them is that they involve demeaning the wrongdoer by seeking to diminish him to a rank that is lower than he now has. Of course the victim may be right to object to the wrongdoer's prideful and inflated sense of his own importance. But such an objection should prompt attempts to correct his sense of his own worth, not to go about trying to prove him or make him lower than he in fact is. If human beings are "treasures beyond price," then trying to damage them in order to make them less valuable, or else representing them as of little value to others, is analogous to defacing the Sistine Chapel, starting a forest fire in Yosemite or ridiculing Chaucer. It is no more right when the victim tries to degrade or falsely diminish the wrongdoer than when the wrongdoer originally degraded or falsely diminished the victim. Those who argue against retribution on the ground that "two wrongs don't make a right" are trying to make this point; they are only wrong to think that retribution is an attempt at such illegitimate degradation or false diminishment.

145

However, there is a much more respectable form of anger that can accompany the desire for retribution. I may feel anger towards my attackers and call them "evil" or "wicked" because I am unable to comprehend why they should have done what they did to me unless they had lost to some significant degree the decency which normally is part of our humanity. Thus I see *them* as "bad." Not just their actions or their character traits but their entire nature as persons takes on an evil cast. The General in Dostoevsky's story seems to be not merely a performer of bad actions but himself a morally repulsive entity. How could one hate the sin but not the sinner in his case? One who would commit such a sin seems so intimately linked with the evil upon which he acts that he seems to be, in and of himself, a kind of sin, irredeemably "rotten." One's opposition to his crime, and the insulting message implicit in that crime, inevitably becomes opposition to *him,* and generates the desire to defeat him and his cause.[34]

I want to argue that moral hatred is the respectable form of hatred that is frequently linked with retribution. Indeed, I want to propose that *what Murphy characterized and defended as retributive hatred is in fact the desire for retribution coupled with the experience of moral hatred of the wrongdoer.* A person who experiences both of these things wants the harm of the wrongdoer for *two* reasons: not only does she want to punish him to vindicate the victim's value, but she also desires (as I suggested in Chapter 2) to hurt him as a way of deterring his evil cause. The punishment becomes a way not only to defeat the wrongdoer in order to annul the message of his crime,

34 Contrast this sense of 'morally bad' with Aristotle's description of some people as "bestial." If I call my assailants "monsters" or "animals" or "beasts" or "psychopaths" I am categorizing them not as immoral but as *horrible.* I am unable to comprehend why they should have done what they did to me unless they have lost to some significant degree their humanity or their sanity. This way of talking about them actually makes them less, rather than more, blameworthy for their actions, and insofar as it characterizes them as non-human, may well represent an attempt on our part to diminish them in order to elevate ourselves (which is malice).

but also to express opposition to (and deter) this enemy of (what she takes to be) morality. And she takes satisfaction in the wrongdoer's suffering, not only because she welcomes the way in which it annuls the demeaning message of his crime, but also because she sees it as a personal defeat for this enemy of morality.

In Chapter 2 I argued that dropping moral hatred and deciding to see the wrongdoer in a favorable light was the essence of the forgiver's change of heart. Thus a "retributive hater," (i.e., a person who morally hates someone she believes deserves retributive punishment) cannot forgive the target of her hatred. *But it is not the desire for retribution which stands in the way of the forgiveness.* One can want to vindicate the value of the victim and still decide to see the wrongdoer (who acted in a way that denied the victim's value) as none-theless decent, and so welcome him back. "I love you and forgive you, but you can't have the car for a week," a parent might say to a wayward teenager. Hence, as we saw in Chapter 2, it is moral hatred which blocks forgiveness, because that hatred involves the belief that this person is (to some degree) a bad thing and an enemy whom one must not welcome back.

So if we want, finally, to determine whether or not Murphy is right to insist that forgiveness is sometimes wrong, we must determine whether or not it is sometimes wrong to give up one's moral hatred of a wrongdoer. And it is to this question that we now turn.

IV. WHEN OUGHT WE TO FORGIVE?

The worry that the practice of forgiveness could actually be damaging to a victim was originally raised by Murphy out of concern that certain psychological preparations necessary for offering forgiveness could be harmful. We have now taken a sustained look at certain aspects of these psychological preparations, and it seems that some of the emotions which must be dropped in order for forgiveness to occur are decidedly *unhealthy*. Murphy might well agree with my argument that we should "overcome," in the sense of *repudiate* malicious or spiteful hatred. But he specifically questioned the idea that we should strive to overcome resentment, which he took to be a reasonable and even healthy emotion.

My analysis of resentment yields only qualified praise for this emotion. Admittedly, a woman who wonders whether she might "deserve" the beatings given her must first bring herself to protest them and challenge the idea that she should receive them before she is in a position to offer genuine forgiveness rather than mere condonation. But resentment is nonetheless an emotion which betrays weakness. Resenters mount a defense against a challenge to their value and rank to which they are in danger of succumbing. Hence their emotion needs to be "overcome" in the sense of *transcended*: they must conquer the fear, inherent in the emotion, that the insulting message in the harmful action is correct. (But how do we go about transcending it? Moral theorists worry about what would count as evidence that other people have value, but is evidence of our own value any easier to find? Is our belief not only in others' value but also in our own value a kind of faith?)

Suppose they do transcend this emotion. They will still experience indignation about the wrongdoing if they drop their defensive posture but sustain their opposition to the action. But I can remain emotionally opposed to someone's action, and still come to be supportive of, even reconciled to, *her*, if I am able to disassociate her from the action and reapprove of her. This is precisely what I cannot do if I morally hate the wrongdoer. And moral hatred does not appear, at first glance, to be something the forgiver ought to be pressured to give up. It seems to be the hallmark of a moral person that she commits herself to, and opposes any attack against, morality. Not to experience indignation at an immoral action, not to have moral hatred for the immoral cause upon which the wrongdoer acted, and not to feel this same aversion towards the wrongdoer himself if he thoroughly identifies himself with that cause, appear to involve giving up one's commitment to the cause of morality.

Despising people such as Ferdinand Marcos or Augusto Pinochet on moral grounds seems appropriate, a way to show the flag under which one is fighting. Nor is it obvious that Jesus, the one who lauds forgiveness, is categorically opposed to this emotion. Indeed, he appears to manifest it on occasion. Although we are expressly forbidden to hate people maliciously or spitefully ("Anyone who nurses anger against his brother must be brought to judgement. If he abuses his brother he must answer for it to the court; if he sneers at him he will have to answer for it in the fires of hell" [Matt. 5:23]), Jesus does appear to encourage us to sustain opposition to our moral opponents, and not to reconcile ourselves with them for as long as they remain committed to their bad cause. ("I have not come to bring peace, but a sword. I have come to set a man against his father, and a daughter against her mother, a son's wife against her mother-in-law; and a man will find his enemies under his own roof" [Matt.10:34–6].)

But Murphy's worries about hatred in Chapter 3 can be understood to caution us not to be too impressed with moral hatred. Take, first of all, his "presumption of judgment" caution. It is essentially a caution against indulging in an emotion whose evaluation of the hated one can easily be *unfair*. Can a moral hater presume to know that the one she hates really is morally wretched? Can she look into the heart of another and know its contents? Indeed, can she be sure of the contents of her own heart so that she knows she is not worse than he? Even if he has done many more overtly immoral acts than she, does she know for sure that her better performance wasn't the result of good fortune rather than fine feeling? Is she sure she would react better had she been subject to the strains and pressures which shaped him? Is her fairly unblemished record a "good" one only by the imperfect standards of her society, and do her past acts of rudeness or indifference or callousness actually signify a worse character than those whose past records include more splashy kinds of crime such as theft, assault, even murder?

The New Testament is filled with warnings for those who

would presume to judge the quality of their assailant's character. Indeed, the evaluation of your assailant as bad may be more of a sign of the poor quality of your soul than of his, insofar as it indicates a readiness not to understand him but to see him as diminished – which is the act not of a moral hater but of a malicious heart. So perhaps malice can be the immoral source of moral hatred.

Second, one must beware of the way in which moral hatred can blind one. It can make one insensitive to aspects of the wrongdoer's character which are not bad, or it can make it hard to understand the way in which his actions are partly a function of pressures and problems which make him more pathetic than evil. I once heard a boy say, after learning that the class bully was in fact a victim of child abuse, "That takes all the fun out of hating her." The boy's reaction to his knowledge shows that it becomes much harder to sustain opposition to wrongdoers as evil enemies when there is evidence that their violence is a reflection of their vulnerability and pathetic circumstances that make their reactions more understandable, and their characters much more like our own.

Wrongdoers are frequently pathetic. Once we understand why they have come to wrong other people, their anger or abuse is often shown to have little to do with the people they in fact hurt, and a lot to do with their own frustrations or feelings of malice towards people they are unable to hurt back, or their sense of powerlessness that is relieved when they are able to succeed in violently coercing others. Our familiarity with the desires and emotions at the base of their immoral actions enables us to see them not as mindless, evil monsters but as human beings like ourselves, with serious problems that ignite feelings of compassion and benevolence.

Note that these feelings are still consistent with the desire that such people experience retribution, showing once again that retribution is not an emotion of hatred towards the offender. Even if I come to pity the bully who beat me up because of her own suffering as a victim of child abuse, I can still insist on the importance of punishing her, not only as a way to deter and morally educate her and anyone else who is aware of the punishment, but more importantly as a way of symbolizing or representing my value relative to hers. And this cause can be taken up by anyone sensitive to the value of human beings, not merely by the victim.

My point is that if we come to know and understand the wrongdoer as an individual, we may retain our hatred of her deeds and of her character traits that led her to hurt another, but still come to feel compassion, and even come to like, the individual herself. And these warmer feelings are what open up the way to forgiveness and reconciliation. Perhaps by calling for love of our enemies Jesus is telling us that such compassion is always possible, no matter how morally wretched a person's actions or character.

Thus Jesus' opposition to the maxim "Love your friends; hate your enemies" may have been opposition *not* to the *lex talionis* or to the principles of retribution, but to the moral hatred of people. Indeed, what marks his moral teaching as distinctive is his encouragement of the idea that despite our immoral actions or traits, we are still not "bad things" to be derisively dismissed or exiled. This thought is also encouraged by the way in which he makes God our "father." As any parent worthy of the name knows, it is difficult to lose completely the sense of your child as special, of worth and inherently good, no matter how wretched he appears. If God sees all of us this way, then how can we dismiss one of our own number as "gone bad"? Aren't we obliged to have faith in a decent core within, even if it is a core which we are completely unable to see?

It may be almost impossible for victims and their friends to take that posture initially. (How could the mother of the boy the General killed think him anything other than a moral monster after the crime?) But as I said in Chapter 2, forgiveness involves seeing the wrongdoer as, despite it all, a person who still possesses decency and one whom we ought to be *for* rather than against.

Moreover, those who are *able* to forgive their wrongdoers are not disabled, by their forgiving posture, from opposing evil, or the evil in human beings. To oppose someone as bad can mean one of two different things: desiring to *repudiate* him or desiring to *correct* him. One who opposes and wants to correct her wrongdoer will experience and convey disapproval of the wrongdoer's action, and disapproval of any of the characteristics from which his action flowed, but still insist that there is a core of decency within him. She will believe, not that he is rotten, but that he has only "cloaked" himself in evil, where his character or dispositions or habits may be taken to be part of the cloak. This belief will allow her to sustain a belief in his inherent decency; removing the evil cloak and reclothing him in something better would allow her to welcome him back into her company.[35] The repudiator, on the other hand, sees the wrongdoer, not merely as cloaked in evil, but as himself a bad thing, and so wants nothing to do with him for as long as he remains "rotted" as an individual. It is this response of repudiation that I have defined as moral hatred, but it isn't the only opposing response open to us.

The inner moral state of a person is notoriously difficult to determine, not only that of others, but also (as Kant reminds us) our own. Evidence garnered from the moral quality of actions isn't decisive proof either way. Thus one may wonder whether Jesus' injunction to "love one's enemies" tells us, in spite of any evidence provided by overt actions or words, to have faith in the inherent decency of all human beings, even those who seem to be the worst among us, so that forgiveness of them after any of their actions is appropriate. This would mean that moral hatred of people – as Augustine's

35 These remarks presuppose that your change of heart towards a wrongdoer can still be consistent with a refusal to renew a relationship with him. Even if you can separate him from his cause, if *he* doesn't separate himself from it, you may be taking a substantial risk that (1) welcoming him back into your company will encourage his commitment (and perhaps others' commitment) to the immoral cause or that (2) welcoming him back will leave you open to further harm (e.g., to your body, your interests or projects, or your loved ones) by this person who has not renounced the ideas, habits or principles that may lead him to inflict such harm.

saying "Hate the sin, not the sinner" suggests – is always wrong because people never become so rotted as individuals that they lose all decency and goodness.

But I admit to having trouble with this counsel. The idea that I should have faith that people such as Dostoevsky's General have some inherent decency despite their actions sticks in my craw. Perhaps God can find enough good in certain highly immoral individuals I have known to forgive them and wash away their crimes, but I confess to finding it beyond me. This confession may place me outside the proper sphere of Christian faith and charity; if so, then there are many like me who *for moral reasons* cannot sustain the charity this religion would require of them.

But does Christianity really require us to maintain such faith in *everyone's* decency? Why should we mortals be required to show God-like generosity, especially when we do not possess God-like access to human hearts? The passages quoted in Section I of this chapter in which Jesus calls the Pharisees (among other things) "vipers" and "white-washed sepulchres . . . full of dead men's bones" suggest that Jesus himself was prepared, on the basis of their behavior, to judge some people as "rotted" beyond hope and fit only for the fires of hell. And the idea that some people might be beyond redemption is certainly part of this religion's tradition, even if it is not currently popular. Jesus' injunction to love one's enemies thus may be intended only to encourage generosity of judgement towards many, not to require it in every case. So, at any rate, I want to propose. Murphy is, to my mind, too ready to withhold forgiveness, but these reflections suggest he is right to insist that there are occasions when it is not morally appropriate – in particular, when too much of the person is "morally dead." Nonetheless that judgement, I have argued, is dangerous, and ought to be resisted for as long as possible.

'Ought' is supposed to imply 'can,' and encouraging or requiring generosity of judgement towards others seems morally reasonable only if such generosity of judgement is possible. Can we judge our assailant to be a decent person if his immoral action against us seems to provide substantial evidence to the contrary? Can there really be an injunction to forgive others, given that this appears to be too much like a command to will a certain (favorable) belief about them?

That injunction makes sense if it is an injunction to drop bad forms of hatred and respond to real evidence of decency on the part of the wrongdoer – for example, her sincere repentance. To manifest decency and "moral health" after a wrongdoing (e.g., through sincere repentance) might be thought to constitute "earning" forgiveness. If the wrongdoer does something to separate herself from the immoral principle or attitude which motivated her action, moral hatred of her no longer seems appropriate, and alienation ought to end.[36]

But what about people who do not repent? Willingness to believe in their decency seems more like self-deception than a genuine change of heart. To the extent that the decision to see another as decent is only covering up a dim assessment of his character based on his assault, that judgement – the heart of moral hatred – can be expected to resurface at some point, perhaps damaging any renewed relationship which the purported forgiveness made possible. Those of us who

---

36 But does such a wrongdoer have a *right* to our forgiveness? I think not; however much her repentance indicates that the victim *ought* to forgive her (so that we think he would be a monster if he did not), such an offer, like any offer of friendship, is a gift which it is the victim's to give; and even if the wrongdoer shows herself worthy of the gift, she cannot be said to have a right to it. Hence, as Murphy notes, the duty to forgive is imperfect, for it cannot be linked with any corresponding right on behalf of the repentant sinner. This point is perhaps made stronger by noting that, even after the wrongdoer has repented, the victim knows there is risk involved in forgiving her, because forgiveness normally culminates in an offer to renew a relationship. Forgiveness may therefore require not only believing that the wrongdoer has sufficient moral worth to justify reacceptance, but also being able to risk being wronged by this person again. So trust may be a precondition of forgiveness. And none of us has a *right* to be trusted. For a discussion of trust, see Annette Baier, "Secular Faith," in her *Postures of the Mind: Essays on Mind and Morals* (Minneapolis: University of Minnesota Press, 1985).

have received "forgiveness" prompted not by conviction based on evidence that we were indeed decent, but by a person's attempt to believe in our decency out of *duty*, know all too well that the reconciliation based on the purported change of heart is unlikely to last, and have felt all the more keenly the sting of the real (dim) judgement against us once it has resurfaced.

Moral or religious theorists who would enjoin us to forgive our wrongdoers would be very unwise if they were in fact demanding that we pretend to have ceased morally hating our assailants. A pretense of forgiving is not a genuine change of heart. Nor does it seem sensible to *try* to have a change of heart. This is surely what Bernard Williams has called "willing to believe," and he has argued that it is self-defeating.[37] But what if this injunction calls us to have faith in another's decency? Having faith in something isn't supposed to be the same as willing to believe it, and is at least arguably not self-defeating. Moreover, having such faith allows us to admit that the behavioral evidence is against decency but to "believe in" the wrongdoer's decency anyhow. (After all, Scripture allows that faith is supposed to involve "unbelief" as much as "belief.")

I am not now equipped with the resources to provide a discourse on the nature of faith. Nonetheless, let me propose that the injunction to forgive is not merely the injunction to encourage in oneself the reapproval of others based on real evidence of decency, but also the injunction to reapprove of others through faith in their decency despite a lack of evidence for it. That is, we are being commanded to defy to ourselves the appearance of these people's rotted souls.

But isn't forgiveness based on such faith frail, even if it has something honest about it (insofar as it admits that the evidence is against decency)? The change of heart arising out of such faith appears to be based more upon what we hope about the wrongdoer's inner character than upon what we

37 See "Deciding to Believe," in Williams's *Problems of the Self* (Cambridge: Cambridge University Press, 1973).

find ourselves ready to believe based upon evidence available to us.

There is one way, however, that the faith upon which forgiveness may rest can be strengthened so that the forgiveness itself is less hesitantly given and less easily undermined. To the extent that we reflect on how the evidence of our *own* actions indicates a poor state of character, then if we would wish for a more generous reading of our character in spite of those actions, we should respect others' wish that we be generous with them. And if we think that, despite what we have done, we *are* still decent human beings, then our faith in ourselves gives us grounds to have faith in others.

These last remarks suggest one final reason for fighting off moral hatred to the extent that it is honestly possible for us to do so. Consider that the admission of moral hatred into the sphere of legitimate response is not only dangerous for the two reasons just discussed (and suggested by Murphy), that is, because it may lead you to believe unfairly that those who have committed wrongdoings are worse than you and because it may blind you to the humane and decent elements within them, but also because it may lead you to *morally hate yourself*. Recall the parable of the unforgiving servant which Murphy quotes near the end of Chapter 1. The master forgives his servant, but the servant in turn goes out and demands full payment from his own debtors. This angers the master, and the servant is severely dealt with as a result. Given that God is supposed to be the master in this tale, one might think that Jesus is telling us that we will be punished to the extent that we aren't charitable, which seems itself a rather uncharitable response to a wrongdoing by a mean-minded and excessively harsh God. But there is another way to read what happens to the servant. How can one who is unable to forgive the sins of others forgive his own sins? The evidence and principles he uses to assess the worthiness of others will, whether he likes it or not, be present when he assesses himself. The more easily he condemns others, the more easily will he be led to condemn himself. "Judge not lest ye be judged" and "As you measure, so will it be meted

156

out to you" are persistent themes of the Gospels, but both, I want to suggest, should be understood to point to the dangerous recoil effect of one's moral evaluations of others. The master doesn't have to throw the unforgiving servant in jail, because the unforgiving servant *places himself there*, along with all the debtors he has condemned. If we are to love ourselves, we must learn to judge others generously. If we allow ourselves to morally hate others, we must guard against morally hating ourselves.

Nonetheless, this argument is not enough to make me repudiate moral hatred altogether. Although moral hatred of oneself is a ghastly experience, accepting that it is what we risk if we decide that moral hatred of others is sometimes a legitimate response may actually encourage our moral improvement. After all, are we not capable of becoming just as morally sick and rotted as other human beings? To admit this to ourselves may serve as a warning to us to avoid making the kinds of choices which lead to potentially irreversible moral rot and the attendant self-disgust.

V. RETRIBUTION AND MERCY

What about retribution itself? Is it a wholly good response on the occasion of any crime, or must we be prepared to give it up in certain circumstances for moral reasons? I want to argue that answering this question involves understanding the difference between forgiveness and mercy, as well as understanding how both are related to punishment.

As I analyzed it, the demand for retribution is the demand for the defeat of the wrongdoer, where his humbling is seen as a way of symbolizing the value of the victim whom he transgressed. But a victim can make this demand and still forgive the wrongdoer. Forgiveness is a change of heart towards the wrongdoer in which one drops any emotions of hatred or resentment towards him and his deed, takes a pro-attitude towards him and is disposed (under most conditions) to make the offer of reconciliation. Since I have analyzed the retributive sentiment as something other than a species of hatred or kind of anger, it is possible, on my analysis, for one to desire retribution and still drop one's resentful, indignant or hateful emotions, and have the change of heart which constitutes forgiveness. Of course, retribution can be and frequently is linked with a form of anger, but one can believe in the appropriateness of this form of vindication of the victim's worth, even if one forgives the wrongdoer. As I noted earlier, it is very common within families for forgiveness and retributive punishment to go hand in hand. I am also told of a remarkable practice in colonial New England to urge a criminal sentenced to hang for his crimes to repent before the event. If he did so, the community would hold a reconciliation feast in his honor, welcoming him back into its midst, but nonetheless it would follow up this feast by hanging him the next day! In this community, reconciliation was not seen as inconsistent with this way of expressing the value of the criminal's victim.[38]

But note that the interests and well-being of the offender do not come into the determination of his "just deserts" except insofar as his very humanity mitigates the sentence that would otherwise be an appropriate expression of the severity of the damage he caused to his victim. And it is when we do pay attention to the offender's well-being that we may decide that mercy rather than further punishment is in order. Whereas forgiveness is a change of heart towards a wrongdoer that arises out of our decision to see him as morally decent rather than bad, *mercy is the suspension or mitigation of a punishment that would otherwise be deserved as retribution, and which is granted out of pity and compassion for the wrongdoer.* What is "deserved" here refers to what is perceived as necessary to humble the wrongdoer and thereby vindicate the victim's value. Given that we are morally

---

38 Note also that forgiveness is not inconsistent with punishment pursued for other purposes. I can welcome you back but punish you if such punishment is a way to deter others, or as a way to complete the moral education I believe you still need despite your progress, which I reward with my renewed friendship.

obliged to annul the wrongdoer's immoral message, this is always a legitimate way of responding to him, assuming that the response is not so severe that it denies his value.

But even if one is always permitted to inflict retributive punishment properly defined and constrained, one can nevertheless be hard-hearted to do so. Like forgiveness, mercy is a *gift* to which the wrongdoer never has a right, but which the punisher may be monstrous not to bestow. The merciful punisher knows full well that he has a "right" to inflict what he has an obligation to inflict, but he also believes himself to have other obligations, in particular, to the wrongdoer as a human being. That is, he is a punisher who is mindful of the victim's right to the reassertion of his value, but he also takes into consideration the effect this symbolic reassertion will have on the wrongdoer himself. For example, consider a murderer who has repented of his crime, suffered profound remorse, and devoted his life to helping the poor in order to atone for his deed. He may deserve life imprisonment if this is taken to be an appropriate expression of the value of the one he killed and not too severe given his own value as a human being. Yet I think that while we would find a system that meted out such a punishment *just*, we would still view it as unacceptably harsh. By virtue of what he had learned and what he had suffered, the punishment would seem to be too *abusive* towards him. Or consider a penitent criminal whose embezzlement had cost him his career, his marriage, his social standing, whose shame had affected his health and whose legal expenses had exhausted his savings. A stiff jail sentence might be expressive of his victims' value, and within the bounds of decent treatment, but a merciful judge might mitigate the sentence out of compassion for the wrongdoer's suffering (although this leniency risks undermining both the deterrent message and the expression of the value the wrongdoer has transgressed).

A deliberation about the appropriateness of merciful treatment must therefore involve the awareness of two different moral parameters. One parameter is the retributive suffering owed by the criminal as an expression of the worth of the one

159

he hurt. The other parameter is the offender's own well-being, which is, of course, different from his worth – which we have already said must always be respected in the construction of a genuinely retributive, rather than vengeful, response. So a judge isn't being merciful if he refrains from torturing a torturer. Choosing another sentence is simply being just; it is a requirement of retribution properly understood. The judge is merciful only when he treats the wrongdoer less severely than is required by retribution properly understood. Punitive treatment that is permissible given the wrongdoer's value may still be badly hurtful or destructive, and if a legal system is sensitive not only to the value but also to the well-being of the one it punishes, it may sometimes choose not to inflict the deserved punishment, out of concern for the harm this may do to him.

Won't every punishment be damaging to an offender's well-being? Of course it will if "damage to well-being" here means the experience of pain, and punishment aiming at the humbling of a wrongdoer generally involves pain. But there are forms of pain that are not bad for our well-being in a broader sense, for instance, the pain associated with childbirth. And as I have argued at length elsewhere,[39] the pain of punishment at least has the potential to be educative to the wrongdoer if he will but listen to the message it carries, so that it has the potential of being good for him. But the examples of abusive (albeit just) punishments I gave earlier were supposed to illustrate situations in which no such educative goal would be effected by the punishment (in large part because the education was already accomplished), or in which the punishment would produce far more bad than good for the offender. These are two situations (there might be others) in which a judge should wonder if he ought to prefer mercy to justice (especially if the wrongdoer's penitent attitude might offset the poor "annulling message" regarding the crime which a punishment less than that required by retributive justice would send).

39 See my "Moral Education Theory of Punishment."

God is said to be merciful, by which I take it that he loves us enough never to punish us in the name of a victim to the point where we are badly hurt or destroyed in the process. Compare God to a parent meting out punishment to a beloved child. Like any parent, he is merciful not because it is just to be so (on the contrary, justice calls for retribution and requires that the offender receive more than God is prepared to mete out), but because his love for the wrongdoer makes it appropriate for him to be so. However, note that his ultimate commitment to justice, if my analysis of retribution is right, would also stem from love – in this case the love of the victim, which includes a deep-seated commitment to the victim's value. So, presumably, in deciding whether or not to be just or merciful, God must balance the competing claims of two of the children He loves. It is a balancing act that families have to perform and it is a balancing act a legal system has to perform if it admits to being interested (as ours seems to do) in the well-being of the offenders it punishes. But the burden of proof would appear to be on the offender to show why justice should not be served; annulling the message of the wrongdoing has high moral priority for a Supreme Being or a legal system committed to the worth of the individuals on whose behalf it punishes. To refrain from annulling that message, or to annul it weakly through a mild punishment, is dangerous both for the cause of morality and for the victim insofar as it may undermine the community's sense of his value and do damage to his self-esteem.

Therefore, to be treated mercifully is to get a gift which we cannot merit, but which arises out of a regard for us that is not contingent on our displaying virtue.[40] If victims insist that such a gift should not be given and that their assailants must receive the punishment that justice (in their name) demands, they endorse a policy of judgement that would rule out their own merciful treatment when it is they who offend. As we measure, so shall we be measured.

40 Note that it is the very heart of Christianity that God's love for us is unconditional in this way.

Chapter 5

Mercy and legal justice

JEFFRIE MURPHY

> I looked at him. Alive. His lap a puddle of blood. With
> the restoration of the normal order of matter and sen-
> sation, I felt I was seeing him for the first time as a
> person. The old human muddles and quirks were set
> flowing again. Compassion, remorse, mercy.
>
> Don DeLillo, *White Noise*

What is the relationship between justice, retribution, resentment, hatred, and revenge? And what is the relationship
between that set of behavioral and emotional responses and
the seemingly opposed promptings of love, charity, and
compassion? I opened an exploration of these questions in
my earlier chapters, and I want to continue it in this chapter
with a discussion of mercy – a virtue (if it is a virtue) that
seems to engage all of the above issues in general and to
raise in particular the issue of the degree to which, if at all,
the demands of justice can be reconciled with the demands
of compassion. If we think of a virtuous person as one
lacking in neither justice nor charity, we will see this reconciliation project as central to an understanding of such matters.

Before beginning this project, however, I want briefly to
consider where, in my view, I now stand with respect to the
thoughts expressed by Jean Hampton. There is no doubt that
we disagree on some important issues and that she has raised
some profound worries that will prompt me to rethink many
of my views. She, for example, sees revenge as inherently

malicious and irrational; and, since what I call retributive hatred involves a desire for revenge, she would reject it too as inherently malicious and irrational. I, however, see revenge (and the hatred that involves a desire for revenge) as a potentially dangerous response but one that is *not* in principle and in all cases inappropriate. And I think (although I am no expert or insider here) that a position similar to mine could be defended as consistent with Christianity. For God Himself seems to promise vengeance to His creatures ("Vengeance is mine; I will repay") while insisting that is improper *for them* to assume the Godly role and presume to exact vengeance themselves. This suggests that (in God's view at any rate) acts of vengeance and revenge are not in principle wrong for *any* being to perform, but are wrong for *finite* and *fallible* beings to perform. (In this way retributive hatred is unlike malice or sadism – dispositions that it would in principle be wrong for any being, even God, to possess.) God, in short, may be viewed as a retributive hater who thinks that no lesser being has a right to join Him in such passions.[1] This is, of course, very like the position I took in Chapter 3. I must admit, though, that my confidence in the views I there expressed – both as philosophical theories and as interpretations of Christianity – has been somewhat shaken by Hampton's remarks.

Recall, however, that our stated goal in this book is not to respond to each other in detail by seeking to refute objections or append additional defenses to our previously stated and defended views. Neither have we attempted to work toward a common view that we can equally endorse. We have decided rather, believing that loose ends are sometimes stimulating and instructive, to leave the disagreements and uncertainties where they stand in the hope that we can use

---

1 If lesser beings may permissibly delight when they sit in Paradise and watch their enemies suffer their promised punishment below in Hell, this will be because they will know that such punishment is now being administered by a morally perfect and omniscient being who may legitimately claim certainty with respect to the judgments he makes in such cases.

each other's work as a starting point toward some new issue or perspective.

Because of this, and because I have the advantage of the last chapter and thus the last word, I am very glad that there is a core of profound agreement between the views I have defended and those defended by Hampton – particularly in her Chapter 4. Although she would not call it hatred and would distinguish its outlet from vengeance or revenge and would give a different ultimate rationale for its expression, she and I agree on this: *There is a legitimate retributive sentiment.* We also agree that this sentiment has something to do both with taking ourselves seriously as bearers of moral rights and with taking wrongdoers seriously as responsible moral agents; and we agree that one legitimate expression of this sentiment may sometimes involve the infliction of suffering (e.g., punishment) on wrongdoers. Moreover, for all of our important differences, we also agree that the ultimate rationale for punishment is to be found not solely in utilitarian considerations (e.g., deterrence, or crime control) but also in considerations of *justice* and what these involve for treating people (including wrongdoers) with the respect that is owed them as responsible moral agents.

Since we both see considerations of justice (including retributive justice) as central to a proper moral outlook, we both are led to mercy as an important but puzzling topic. Mercy, grounded in love (charity) and compassion, initially seems inconsistent with justice; for to treat a person with mercy may involve giving him less than his just deserts. On the other hand, if the virtuous person is one who exemplifies both justice and charity in his character, then these two considerations must ultimately be consistent – perhaps, even, as Hampton suggests, simply different aspects of the same value. Thus, since the topic of mercy is one to which we are both naturally led by our previous reflections, it will be a fitting topic on which to close our book. I will thus attempt to address the issues that Hampton raised at the close of the preceding chapter and develop an account of mercy – its relation to justice, its proper role in the life of a

virtuous person, and its proper role in institutionalized justice: the law.

I. MERCY AND THE CRIMINAL LAW

We are ordinarily inclined to believe that both justice and
mercy are moral virtues. We are also inclined to maintain that
both of these virtues are characteristics of such lofty objects
as God and of such human, all too human objects as legal
systems – where in literature and folklore we celebrate (perhaps without fully understanding what we are saying) those
judges who can "temper their justice with mercy." As we
expect God as cosmic judge to manifest both justice and
mercy, so too do we expect this of secular judges. Or so we
often say. For example, Shakespeare's two important "com-
edies of mercy," *Measure for Measure* and *The Merchant of
Venice*, contain some of the most often quoted sentiments on
mercy and justice in our civilization:

> The quality of mercy is not strain'd;
> It droppeth as the gentle rain from heaven
> Upon the place beneath: it is twice blessed;
> It blesseth him that gives and him that takes:
> 'Tis mightiest in the mightiest; it becomes
> The throwned monarch better than his crown;
> His sceptre shows the force of temporal power,
> The attribute to awe and majesty,
> Wherein doth sit the dread and fear of kings;
> But mercy is above this scepter'd sway, –
> It is enthroned in the heart of kings,
> It is an attribute to God himself;
> And earthly power doth then show likest God's
> When mercy seasons justice.
> (*The Merchant of Venice*, IV, Portia speaks)

> No ceremony that to great ones 'longs,
> Not the king's crown, nor the deputed sword,
> The marshall's truncheon, nor the judge's robe,
> Become them with one half so good a grace

As mercy does.
(*Measure for Measure*, II, Isabella speaks)

These passages express some fairly widely held – and closely related – views about mercy: (1) It is an autonomous moral virtue (i.e., not reducible to some other virtue – especially justice). (2) It is a virtue that tempers or "seasons" justice – something one adds to justice (the primary virtue) to dilute it and perhaps, if one takes the metallurgical metaphor of tempering seriously, to make it stronger. (3) It is never owed to anyone as a right or a matter of desert or justice. It always therefore transcends the realm of strict moral obligation and is best viewed as a free gift – an act of grace, love, or compassion that is beyond the claims of right, duty, and obligation. ("The quality of mercy is not [con-] strained.") (4) As a moral virtue, it derives its value at least in part from the fact that it flows from a certain kind of character – a character disposed to perform merciful acts from love or compassion while not losing sight of the importance of justice. (5) It requires a generally retributive outlook on punishment and responsibility. Mercy is often regarded as found where a judge, out of compassion for the plight of a particular offender, imposes upon that offender a hardship less than his just deserts. This way of conceptualizing mercy requires, of course, that we operate with a rich concept of "just desert" – not easy to come by on a utilitarian/ deterrence analysis.[2]

All this suggests that there are certain other virtues or at least desiderata of moral and legal systems with which mercy often is but should not be confused: excuse, justification, and forgiveness. If a person has actually done the right thing (i.e., if his conduct was justified) or if he was not responsible for what he did (i.e., had a valid excuse), then it would simply be unjust to punish him, and no question of mercy need arise

2 Note that this is a list of commonly held views about mercy and its relation to justice. I am not at this point necessarily endorsing any of them.

– for there is no responsible wrongdoing, and responsible wrongdoing is (it is commonly thought) the proper object of mercy.

Forgiveness is trickier. According to the view I developed in Chapter 1, forgiveness is primarily a matter of changing how one feels with respect to a person who has done one an injury. (Hampton sees this as a prelude to forgiveness; I see it as the very thing.) It is, in my view, particularly a matter of overcoming, on moral grounds, the resentment a self-respecting person quite properly feels when suffering such an injury. Mercy, though related to forgiveness, is clearly different in at least these two respects. First, to be merciful to a person requires not merely that one change how one feels about that person but also a specific kind of action (or omission) – namely, treating that person less harshly than, in the absence of the mercy, one would have treated him. Second, it is not a requirement of my showing mercy that *I* be an injured party. All that is required is that I stand in a certain relation to the potential beneficiary of mercy. This relation – typically established by legal or other institutional rules – makes it appropriate that I impose some hardship upon the potential beneficiary of mercy.

Although these common views about the virtue of mercy seem plausible on the surface, they are in fact deeply paradoxical. For the following pattern of argument seems tempting: If mercy requires a tempering of justice, then there is a sense in which mercy may require a departure from justice. (Temperings are tamperings.) Thus to be merciful is perhaps to be unjust. But it is a vice, not a virtue, to manifest injustice. Thus mercy must be, not a virtue, but a vice – a product of morally dangerous sentimentality. This is particularly obvious in the case of a sentencing judge. We (society) hire this individual to enforce the rule of law under which we live. We think of this as "doing justice," and the doing of this is surely his sworn obligation. What business does he have, then, ignoring his obligations to justice while he pursues some private, idiosyncratic, and not publicly accountable virtue of love or compassion?[3] Shakespeare, always sensitive to both sides of complex moral issues, captures this thought well, even in the midst of his dramatic sermons on mercy:

> I show [pity] most of all when I show justice,
> For then I pity those I do not know,
> Which a dismissed offense would after gall;
> And do him right that, answering one foul wrong,
> Lives not to act another.
>
> *(Measure for Measure*, II, Angelo speaks)

The point here, I take it, is that the judge who is influenced simply by the plight of the offender before him may lose sight of the fact that his job is to uphold an entire system of justice that protects the security of all citizens.

Perhaps the clearest statements of the paradoxes I want to develop on mercy come from Saint Anselm. His worry is about the divine nature – how can God be both just and merciful? – but the paradoxes he formulates can easily be adapted to secular and legal concerns. He writes:

> What justice is it that gives him who merits eternal death everlasting life? How, then, gracious Lord, good to the wicked, can you save the wicked if this is not just, and you do nothing that is not just? (*Proslogium* IX)

and

3 Note that I describe the judge's job as that of upholding the *rule of law*. I mean by this the upholding of legal rules that meet certain standards of justice, not the mechanical upholding of any legal rules at all no matter how unjust they may be. Of course I do not believe that judges should enforce legal rules in the absence of any reflection on the merits of those rules from the point of view of justice. If the rules are unjust, then – if the judge has discretion – he should use that discretion to do justice. (If the judge has no discretion and if the rules are terribly unjust, then such drastic acts as resignation or civil disobedience may be in order.) These complexities, however, do not show a need for a special virtue of mercy; and only a highly impoverished view of justice (i.e., that it is simply the mechanical following of rules) would make one think that these complexities could not be dealt with in terms of a sophisticated theory of justice – such as the theory of "judicial integrity" developed by Ronald Dworkin in *Law's Empire* (Cambridge, Mass.: Harvard University Press, 1986).

But if it can be comprehended in any way why you can will to save the wicked, yet by no consideration can we comprehend why, of those who are alike wicked, you save some rather than others, through supreme goodness, and why you condemn the latter, rather than the former, through supreme justice. (*Proslogium* XI)

Although Anselm's specific worry is about the divine nature (are the divine attributes of perfect justice and perfect compassion coherently ascribable to the same being?), he raises a general worry about the concepts of justice and mercy themselves – namely, to what degree (if at all) are they consistent? More specifically, if we simply use the term "mercy" to refer to certain of the demands of justice (e.g., the demand for individuation), then mercy ceases to be an autonomous virtue and instead becomes a part of (is reducible to a part of) justice. It thus becomes obligatory, and all the talk about gifts, acts of grace, supererogation, and compassion becomes quite beside the point. If, on the other hand, mercy is totally different from justice and actually requires (or permits) that justice sometimes be set aside, it then counsels injustice. In short, mercy is either a vice (injustice) or redundant (a part of justice). (This is a gloss on Anselm's first paradox – from IX. The second paradox – from XI – will be explored a bit later.)

II. MERCY AS JUSTICE

In an interesting article on mercy, Alwynne Smart seeks to establish that there is indeed a place for mercy in a world that takes the value of justice seriously, and she develops her discussion of this general issue in terms of specific cases – cases that are supposed to test and hone our intuitions so that we can be in "reflective equilibrium" about the issues of justice and mercy.[4]

4 Alwynne Smart, "Mercy," in *The Philosophy of Punishment*, ed. H. B. Acton (New York: St. Martin's Press, 1969), pp. 212–27. (Smart's article originally appeared in *Philosophy*, October 1968.) Another important

Smart asks that we consider the following pairs of cases –
cases that might face a sentencing judge (who, we may suppose, has some discretion and is not bound by mandatory
sentencing rules):

A	*B*
1. The defendant, convicted of vehicular homicide, had his own child – whom he loved deeply – as his victim.	The defendant has been convicted of killing another person in cold blood.
2. The defendant is a young and inexperienced criminal.	The defendant is a hardened career criminal.

According to Smart, we would all agree that the judge
should impose a lighter sentence on those persons under *A*
than on those under *B* and that it would be proper, in a perfectly ordinary sense of the word "mercy," to express our
conviction about what he should do by saying that he should
show mercy in those cases.

Let us suppose that Smart is correct. It is proper for the
judge to go easy here, and such easing up would be called by
many people an act of mercy. This still strikes me as philo-
sophically confused and as an obstacle to philosophical clar-
ity on the concept of mercy. If we feel that the judge should
go easy on cases under *A*, this is surely because we believe
that there is some morally relevant feature that distinguishes
these cases from those under *B*. What might this feature be?
In example *A*1, it is no doubt our conviction that the criminal

article is Claudia Card's "Mercy," *Philosophical Review*, 81 (April 1972),
pp. 182–207. Since Smart's article provides me with a useful starting
point for what I want to say about mercy, I focus my discussion on her
piece and do not give Card's the attention it deserves. Card, like Smart,
operates within what I will later call the criminal law paradigm (a paradigm I will reject for mercy), and, also like Smart, she seems to offer
a view of mercy that makes it a part of justice (on a sophisticated theory
of justice) and not an autonomous moral virtue.

The cases Jean Hampton discusses in her brief section on mercy in
Chapter 4 (the repentant and reformed murderer and the embezzler
whose crime brings disaster onto himself) are very analogous to two of
the cases raised by Smart – cases I shall discuss in this section.

has already suffered a great deal – perhaps even that he has suffered enough – and that the infliction of any additional misery by the state would be gratuitous and cruel. In example *A*2, we are no doubt influenced by the idea that the character of a younger person is less mature and thus less responsible than that of a hardened criminal.[5] But, if this is our thinking, then why talk of mercy here and confuse what we are doing with some moral virtue that requires the tempering of justice? For to avoid inflicting upon persons more suffering than they deserve, or to avoid punishing the less responsible as much as the fully responsible, is a simple – indeed obvious – demand of justice. Basic demands of justice are that like cases be treated alike, that morally relevant differences between persons be noticed, and that our treatment of those persons be affected by those differences. This demand for individuation – a tailoring of our retributive response to the individual natures of the persons with whom we are dealing – is a part of what we mean by taking persons seriously as persons and is thus a basic demand of justice. One could introduce a sense of "mercy" that means "seeking to tailor our response to morally relevant individual differences." But this would be confusing and dangerous – confusing because it would make us think that the rich literature noted above (Shakespeare, Anselm) was somehow relevant to this, dan-

---

5 Perhaps we also think that prison will be harder on them and hence that they may suffer more than they deserve. Perhaps we might also think that young people are more likely to be influenced by the bad environment that prison represents.

 The idea that it is immoral to impose a level of suffering out of proper proportion to a person's character is also central to Card's view of mercy (see note 4, this chapter). She writes (p. 184): "Mercy ought to be shown to an offender when it is evident that otherwise (1) he would be made to suffer unusually more on the whole, owing to his peculiar misfortunes, than he deserves in view of his basic character and (2) he would be worse off in this respect than those who stand to benefit from the exercise of their right to punish him (or have him punished). When the conditions of this principle are met, the offender deserves mercy." Card thus seems explicitly to classify merciful acts as a subcategory of just acts, and not as acts autonomous from justice. But I fail to understand how she can then say (also on p. 184) that "desert of mercy does not give rise to an obligation."

gerous because it might lead us to suppose that individuation is not owed to persons as a right and is thus somehow optional as a free gift or act of grace. But this would be deeply wrong. The legal rules, if they are just, will base required penal treatment on morally relevant differences, or they will give judges the discretion to do so; and criminal defendants surely have a right that it be this way.[6] One could talk of mercy here, but why? (One might as well protest strict criminal liability offenses by saying that they are unmerciful.) Judges or lawmakers who are unmindful of the importance of individuational response are not lacking in mercy; they lack a sense of justice.[7] Recall our earlier dilemma: Mercy either is a vice or is redundant. These cases illustrate redundancy.

Smart is sensitive to the fact that not everyone will find her initial cases representative of mercy in any deep or interesting sense, and she thus introduces some additional cases in an attempt to capture a different and more important kind of mercy. These are cases where (unlike in the earlier cases) we agree that some punishment P is, all relevant things about Jones considered, the just punishment for what Jones has done. Still, on moral grounds, we argue that a punishment less than P should be inflicted. We now have a virtue that is not redundant – is not merely reducible to justice. These are the cases:

6 In commenting on an earlier draft of this chapter, Lewis Beck raised the question of how the demand for individuation (which I suggest is a demand of justice) can be squared with the common and intuitively compelling metaphor that "justice is blind." The short answer, I think, is that justice is not to be totally blind but is, rather, to be blind to all aspects of an individual that have no bearing on the question of what his just deserts really are – blind to such matters as race, sexual attractiveness and willingness, or ability to bribe.

7 Those who desire to talk about mercy in this context probably do so because they have an overrestricted and simplistic conception of justice and thus fail to appreciate all that would be involved in a sophisticated theory of retributive justice and the role of the judiciary in implementing such a theory. Let us be clear about this: If a person has a valid excuse or justification for what he has done, then he has not engaged in responsible wrongdoing, and it is therefore *unjust* to punish him.

3. Jones's family, who need his support very much, would be harmed to an unacceptable degree if *P* is inflicted on Jones. Therefore a judge ought to show mercy to Jones and inflict less than *P*.
4. Adverse social consequences will result if *P* is inflicted on Jones. (Perhaps he is a popular leader of the political opposition, and his followers will riot or commit acts of terrorism if *P* is inflicted on Jones.) Therefore a judge should show mercy to Jones.
5. Jones has been in jail for a long time and has so reformed that he is, in a very real sense, a "new person." Therefore a judge (or other appropriate official) should show him mercy and grant him an early release.

I find these cases unpersuasive. It strikes me as analytic that mercy is based on a compassionate concern for the *defendant's* plight, and this feature is absent in cases 3 and 4. If we are showing mercy to anyone in case 3 it is to Jones's family, and he is simply the indirect beneficiary of the mercy. But even this seems a confusing way to talk. In cases 3 and 4 one is basically choosing to bring about a net gain in utility. This may be reasonable if a utilitarian moral outlook is reasonable. But these cases would not be interestingly unique given that outlook; and, not placing great moral weight on the concept of just desert anyway, it is not an outlook in which a concern with mercy as a special virtue is likely to arise.

Case 5 is, of course, very different. But it, like Smart's earlier cases, seems simply a matter of justice. I am suspicious of "new person" talk. However, if there really are cases where we should take it literally, then it is obviously a matter of justice that one does not punish one person for the crimes of another. Why talk of mercy here?

In summary: We have yet to find one case of genuine mercy as an autonomous virtue. The cases we have explored represent either unjustified sentimentality, virtuous behavior that is simply a matter of justice, or situations where the demands of justice are thought to be overridden by the demands of utility. Hence some skepticism about mercy seems in order. Judges in criminal cases are obligated to do justice.[8] So too, I would argue, are prosecutors and parole boards in their exercise of discretion.[9] There thus simply is no room for mercy as an autonomous virtue with which their justice should be tempered. Let them keep their sentimentality to themselves for use in their private lives with their families and pets.

III. PRIVATE LAW AND A NEW PARADIGM FOR MERCY

But surely this is too quick. Could all the rich and moving literature of mercy really be totally worthless – nothing but propaganda for mindless sentimentality? I think not, and I shall spend the remainder of this chapter attempting to think about

8 Recall that by this claim I do not mean that judges are always obligated to enforce any rule no matter how unjust that rule may be. My point is rather this: The focus of a judge, either in enforcing a rule or in seeking a way to modify or get around it, is to be on the question of what is required by justice – not on what he may be prompted out of compassion to do. "I personally feel sorry for you" should never, in my opinion, be offered by a judge as a ground in sentencing; for a judge sits as representative of the rule of law, not as representative of his own feelings.

9 Special problems may arise for a chief executive or head of state in his exercise of the power of pardon. The "job description" for such an office may, to borrow some language from Aquinas, involve a concern for the common good or common welfare of the community in the executive's care. This might mean that, in deciding whether to pardon an individual, the chief executive (unlike a trial judge) might legitimately draw upon values other than the requirements of justice and thus might legitimately ignore the just deserts of an individual and pardon that individual if the good of the community required it. This whole account, of course, presupposes a political theory of the various offices and roles required by society and a theory of the proper values and decision-making criteria proper to (and perhaps unique to) each of the offices and roles. Space does not allow the articulation, much less the defense, of such a theory in the present context. Even with respect to the chief executive, however, Kant's caution against pardon is surely in order: "The right to pardon a criminal, either by mitigating or by entirely remitting the punishment, is certainly the most slippery of all the rights of the sovereign. By exercising it he can demonstrate the splendor of his majesty and yet thereby wreak injustice to a high degree" (*Metaphysical Elements of Justice*, trans. John Ladd [Indianapolis: Bobbs-Merrill, 1965], pp. 107–8).

mercy in a different way – one that may allow us to give it some meaningful life as an autonomous moral virtue.[10]

Thus far we have been operating with what might be called the "criminal law paradigm" of mercy – thinking of mercy as a virtue that most typically would be manifested by a sentencing judge in a criminal case. This is the paradigm represented in *Measure for Measure* where Isabella begs Angelo, a judge in a criminal case involving her brother, to show her brother mercy. It is this paradigm, I have suggested, that is probably a failure.

But there is another paradigm, as represented in *The Merchant of Venice*, that I will call the "private law paradigm." In that play, you will recall, the central focus is on a civil case – a contract dispute. Antonio has made a bad bargain with Shylock and, having defaulted, is contractually obligated to pay Shylock a pound of his flesh. Portia, acting as judge, asks that Shylock show mercy to Antonio by not demanding the harsh payment.[11]

Note how radically this case differs from the criminal law case. A judge in a criminal case has an *obligation* to do justice – which means, at a minimum, an obligation to uphold the rule of law. Thus if he is moved, even by love or compassion, to act contrary to the rule of law – to the rules of justice – he acts wrongly (because he violates an obligation) and manifests a vice rather than a virtue. A criminal judge, in short, has an obligation to impose a just punishment; and all of his discretion within the rules is to be used to secure greater justice (e.g., more careful individuation). No rational society would write any other "job description" for such an important institutional role.

But a litigant in a civil suit is not the occupier – in anything like the same sense – of an institutional role. He occupies a private

10 The following discussion is greatly influenced by P. Twambley's important article "Mercy and Forgiveness," *Analysis*, (January 1976), pp. 84–90.
11 Portia serves a complex role in the play. She does not simply represent the virtue of mercy but also stands as a representative of hypocrisy, unjust manipulation, and anti-Semitism.

role. He does not have an antecedent obligation, required by the rules of justice, to impose harsh treatment. He rather has, in a case like Shylock's, a *right* to impose harsh treatment. Thus, if he chooses to show mercy, he is simply waiving a right that he could in justice claim – not violating an obligation demanded by justice.[12] (Recall my example in Chapter 1 of the rules of chivalric combat. The fallen knight begs for mercy. He asks not that the victor violate an obligation to kill him but, rather, that the victor show pity or compassion and waive a right to kill him.) And there is no contradiction, paradox, or even tension here. I do not necessarily show a lack of respect for justice by waiving my justice-based rights as I would by ignoring my justice-derived obligations.[13] Thus, in the private law paradigm, the virtue of mercy is revealed when a person, out of compassion for the hard position of the person who owes him an obligation, waives the right that generates the obligation and frees the individual of the burden of that obligation. People who are always standing on their rights, indifferent to the impact this may have on others, are simply intolerable. Such persons cannot be faulted on grounds of justice, but they can certainly be faulted. And the disposition to mercy helps to check these narrow and self-involved tendencies present in each of us. There is thus room for mercy as an important moral virtue with impact upon the law, but it is a virtue to be manifested by private persons using the law – not by officials enforcing the law.[14]

12 There may be special problems in cases (defamation perhaps) where tort suits aid in upholding certain socially important rules and protections. In this sense they are not purely private legal matters even though they are handled in the private law rather than in the criminal law. Thus there may be cases where an individual might feel a public responsibility to proceed with a private lawsuit.

13 I say "not necessarily" because there are cases where a refusal to stand on one's rights and demand just treatment would reveal a lack of self-respect and a lack of respect for oneself as a morally relevant object (and thus a lack of respect for the rules of morality themselves). This was, you will recall, a central argument of Chapter 1. Of course, not every case of standing on one's rights (no matter how trivial) is of this nature.

14 Should judges in civil cases sometimes follow Portia's lead and encourage litigants to show mercy? Perhaps; but there are problems

Note also that this private law paradigm might help, by analogy, with Anselm's theological puzzle about mercy. Anselm sees a paradox in attributing both justice and mercy to God because he seems to see God as analogous to a judge in a criminal case – as someone with an obligation to enforce certain rules. But surely this is not the only model of God. God (at least on one fairly common view) is not bound by independent rules of obligation with respect to His creatures; for the rules of morality are, on this view, simply His commands. He does, however, have many rights with respect to His creatures. Thus His mercy may be viewed as His deciding, out of love or compassion, to waive certain rights that He has – not to violate certain obligations that He has. Anselm's first paradox disappears.

IV. A RETURN TO THE CRIMINAL LAW

If crimes are offenses against the state, and if the state is nothing but a collection of private individuals, and if individuals may legitimately – as I have argued – sometimes show mercy by waiving rights that they have, then perhaps my earlier strictures against mercy in the criminal law need to be rethought.[15] Consider the possible situation that Peter Westen has raised with me in correspondence: Assume that having learned that a judge has sentenced a public official to jail for using public funds – along with his own personal funds – to feed homeless children without city approval and in violation of a city ordinance, the townspeople unanimously, by acclamation, enact an ordinance pardoning him

here. The peaceable desire to settle cases and avoid the human and financial costs of acrimonious litigation is certainly an understandable one; but, as Jules Coleman and Charles Silver argue, there are serious social costs involved in settlement as well – e.g., the cost of not having the law clarified in the way that actual litigation makes possible. See Jules Coleman and Charles Silver,"Justice in Settlements," *Social Philosophy and Policy*, 4 (Autumn 1986), pp. 102–44.

15 This section was written in response to comments by Peter Westen and Antony Duff on an earlier draft of this chapter. I doubt, however, that it goes far enough in meeting the profound worries they raised.

for his offense. If each citizen can justly exercise mercy individually when his individual interests are at issue, why may not all citizens justly join together and exercise mercy collectively when their collective interests are at issue? And if they may do this by statute, may they not call on the governor to pardon? And if they may call on the governor to pardon in a particular case, may they not simply *delegate* to the governor (or to the *judiciary*) the power to exercise mercy on their behalf whenever he believes that they would, out of love and compassion, so desire – even if they have not petitioned and even if they are not unanimous on the issue?

This is a fascinating problem, and it merits a complex response – a response that will involve a partial recantation of my previous claim that no room can be found for the virtue of mercy in the criminal law. At the outset, however, I think it worth noting that this may not be a pure case of mercy. For perhaps in this situation the people are in part motivated by a belief that the defendant, in some sense, *did the right thing*. Our uneasiness about punishing those whose lawbreaking is conscientiously motivated (e.g., civil disobedients) seems to me to raise concerns that, though very important, are other than mercy. Suppose that a majority of people felt sorry for, and wanted to show mercy toward, an individual whose crime had been the violation of the civil rights of some racial minority. Would we be inclined to look so favorably on this case?

The problem of protecting minorities and other victims can be avoided, of course, if we require that the desire to show mercy be unanimous;[16] and, in such a case, I am now prepared to admit that Westen is correct in principle – that in

16 Since *rights* are involved, some kind of *unanimity* would seem to be required or at least desirable – if not actual unanimity, then perhaps projected hypothetical unanimity of all rational persons or at least all rational immediate victims. Just as constitutional rights are supposed to be checks on representative democracy and not merely expressions of it, so would legitimate waivers of the rights of victims require appeal to values other than those found in the idea of representative majority rule.

principle mercy may find a legitimate home in the criminal law. This home can be seen, however, only when we see the criminal law through the private law model I have previously developed; for, given an extension of this model, why should not each citizen be allowed to waive his right that a guilty person be punished? If, as seems likely, the answer is *no reason*, then the only question remaining is that of which state agency is appropriate to act out the general will. I am still convinced that a judge would be acting wrongly in principle in showing mercy on the basis of his own *personal* sympathy or compassion. Such a judge would be violating an obligation in that he would be letting *his feelings* prompt him to waive *our rights*. But if a judge can be viewed (to use a phrase suggested by Jean Hampton) as taking on the personae of all of us (including our feelings), then we – through him – would be waiving our own rights. And this, as I have argued in developing the private law model, is typically not problematical at all.

Now it is, of course, problematical that it is correct (or even intelligible) to view any official as taking on our personae – as representing our feelings – in such matters. And even if a case can be made for such a way of thinking, it is still not obvious that a *judge* (as opposed to some other official) is the appropriate one vicariously to waive our rights. Recall, for example, that I earlier (note 9) expressed a preference for the executive and the power of pardon over any mercy role for the judiciary – partly because of the executive's high visibility and more immediate accountability. (In the American system, one may be thankful, there are no chief executives with life tenure in their jobs.) However, such matters, important as they are, pertain more to institutional design than to basic moral principle. And on the issue of basic principle, I am now prepared to admit this: Since individuals may legitimately show mercy in waiving their rights, a judge or any other official may exercise mercy in a criminal case *if* (and this is a very big "if") it can be shown that such an official is acting, not merely on his own sentiments, but as a vehicle for expressing the sentiments of all those who have been victimized by the criminal and who, given those sentiments, wish to waive the right that each has that the criminal be punished.

That I am now willing to put the point in this way shows that I am now inclined to defend a much weaker form of retributivism than I defended in the past. For now, having been finally beaten into submission by repeated arguments from Jean Hampton and others (thereby receiving, no doubt, my just deserts), I am no longer inclined to argue that justice *requires* that criminals suffer retributive punishment. Rather, I am now drawn to a weaker view: that justice *allows* or *permits* this, that demanding it (if one is a victim) is a *right* but not a duty. To return to a theme in my chapter on hatred: A person may legitimately feel retributive hatred when wronged by another and may legitimately act on such a feeling – by seeking revenge – if able to satisfy all the constraints and cautions to such action that I developed. But this person is not required to have such feelings, nor is he required, if he has them, to act on them. He simply acquires a right – one which he may waive without criticism so long as his reasons for so doing are noble rather than the base (e.g., compassion or a desire to reform the offender rather than timidity, cowardice, or lack of self-respect).

V. MERCY AND EQUAL PROTECTION

Is everything now coherent in the land of mercy? Is its status as an autonomous virtue, different from and tempering justice, intact – ready to be dispensed from our compassionate natures as a free gift or act of grace? Not quite. For Anselm's second paradox now appears to haunt us:

> But if it can be comprehended in any way why you can will to save the wicked, yet by no consideration can we comprehend why, of those who are alike wicked, you save some rather than others, through supreme goodness, and why you condemn the latter, rather than the former, through supreme justice. (*Proslogium* XI)

Anselm here seems to be raising a kind of "equal protection" paradox: If God (or any other rational being) shows mercy, then the mercy must not be arbitrary or capricious but must rather rest upon some good reason – some morally relevant feature of the situation that made the mercy seem appropriate. Compassion and love are, after all, cognitively loaded emotions; they are not sensations like headaches or tickles. Thus they are the sorts of reactions for which reasons may be given; and where reasons are given, it is possible to distinguish good from bad reasons, relevant from irrelevant ones. ("I showed him mercy because he was so sick" has a kind a sense lacking in "I showed him mercy because he was so handsome.") But once a reason always a reason. And does not the Principle of Sufficient Reason require that if I, as a rational being, showed mercy to Jones because of characteristic C, then it is presumably required of me (*rationally* required, not just morally required) that I show comparable mercy to C-bearing Smith?[17] But, if so, then what becomes of all this grace/free gift talk when applied to mercy? Is it nothing more than this: I am never required to show mercy; but if I slip and show it even once, then I am rationally required to show it to all relevantly similar persons? This does not seem correct. If there are good reasons for mercy – relevant features that ought to incline the mind – they will be and remain good reasons whether they are acted on or not. Thus some of Anselm's second paradox remains.

VI. THE FOUNDATIONS OF MERCY

Let me close my discussion of mercy with one very tentative exploration.[18] Up to now I have been playing with what I think are widely shared ordinary intuitions about mercy,

---

17 For a discussion of the Principle of Sufficient Reason (a rational being will not prefer one thing to another without basing that preference on some relevant difference between the things) and equal protection, see my "Justifying Departures from Equal Treatment," *Journal of Philosophy*, 81 (October 1984), pp. 587–93.
18 I owe much of the following to discussions with Ray Elugardo.

justice, resentment, love, and compassion – trying to attain that nirvana of moral epistemology that Rawls calls "reflective equilibrium." But it might be worth exploring some questions of a more foundational nature. No doubt most of us do see justice as the primary value with respect to law, but we also want to find someplace for mercy as a secondary virtue to temper or otherwise have some effect on justice. It is interesting to inquire into why we think this and whether our common pattern of thought is rationally justified.

Let us suppose for a moment that Gilbert Harman is at least partly correct about ethics: At least some of our moral views are simply conventions that result from tacit bargains struck between the weak and poor and the rich and powerful – bargains in which each attempts to maximize his self-interest while still securing the vital benefits of social cooperation.[19] This might be a start toward explaining some of our ordinary views about justice and mercy. Justice – the regular enforcement of the rules that make social stability (and thus social life) possible – will be a strong priority of all parties to the bargain – whether rich or poor, strong or weak. Not all will have the same stake in these rules, but all (or almost all) will have a high stake. Thus it is not difficult to see why conventions of justice should have a high priority. Mercy, however, is a different matter. It is more likely to be needed by the poor and weak than by the rich and powerful, and thus it is easy to see why it is present (some level of it is perhaps required to secure the cooperation and compliance of the disadvantaged) but also easy to see why it does not have the dominant role that justice has – why it only tempers justice but never replaces or supersedes it.

The bargaining model of moral conventions might also provide a start toward dealing with Anselm's second paradox – namely, if I show mercy to C-bearing Jones, how can I consistently (morally?) fail to show mercy to equally C-bearing

---

19 Gilbert Harman, "Justice and Moral Bargaining," *Social Philosophy and Policy*, 1 (Autumn 1983), pp. 114–31. Similar views may also be found in such otherwise diverse thinkers as Hume, Marx, and Nietzsche.

Smith? If moral conventions are viewed as agreements based on rational self-interest, then the impact *on me* of my continued showings of mercy would become relevant. Thus what relevantly distinguishes the Jones case from the Smith case will not be some feature that distinguishes Jones from Smith but rather some feature that distinguishes the impact *on me* of mercy to Jones from the impact *on me* of mercy to Smith. The mere fact that Jones got there first (or I noticed him first) might then make a great deal of difference. I show mercy to Jones, who is pitiful to degree P, and thus forgive his debt to me of five dollars. Smith, who is also pitiful to degree P, also owes me five dollars. I do not show him mercy, however, because – though I can afford the loss of five dollars – I cannot afford the loss of ten. Also, I may begin to fear – quite legitimately – that if I start to make a practice of showing mercy, instead of simply showing it every now and then when the spirit moves me, I will be taken for an easy mark in future dealings with those who might attempt to exploit my perceived goodwill. Thus, if rational persons thought that once having shown mercy they would be stuck with making a regular practice of it, they might be inclined never to show it at all. But since, as I have argued, there are reasons why rational agents would agree to conventions establishing some level of mercy, they would not want to adopt a principle of mercy that would give rational persons incentives never to show it. And therefore they would probably agree with the adoption of mercy as what Kant called an imperfect duty – a duty that admits of wide latitude in the time and manner of its fulfillment.[20]

20 This pattern of argument for an imperfect duty of mercy bears some
    interesting analogies to Kant's argument for the imperfect duty of
    benevolence. Kant argues as follows: Given that I would want others
    to come to my aid if I needed them, and given that there is a non-trivial
    possibility that I might someday need the aid of others, it would be
    irrational for me to will membership in a world where no duty at all to
    help others in distress is recognized. On the other hand, no rational
    person would want to be a hostage to all the misfortunes of all other
    people – a concern which helps explain why the duty will be only
    imperfect. For a stimulating argument that Kantian conclusions can be

VII. CONCLUDING REMARKS

> The eyes of philosophers see through the opaqueness of the
> world, eliminate the flesh of it, reduce the variety of existing
> things to a spider's web of relationships between general ideas,
> and fix the rules according to which a finite number of pawns
> moving on a chessboard exhaust a number of combinations
> that may even be infinite.
>
> Italo Calvino, "Philosophy and Literature"

I have now come to the end of my ruminations on the topics
of resentment, hatred, forgiveness, compassion, and mercy.
I have suggested that there is more to be said for hatred and
resentment than many people will admit (and that the virtue
of forgiveness is thus a qualified one) and somewhat less to
be said in favor of compassion and mercy than is often
claimed. As I read back over what I have written, however,
I am painfully aware of two things: how *personal* (and thus
very likely limited) my perspective on these matters is and
how unlikely it is that the full, rich texture of such topics as
forgiveness and mercy is to be totally captured in the logical
structures where I have attempted to confine and understand
them. I was born a natural hater (is this genetic with the
Irish?),[21] and I was also subjected to a classic Protestant

generated from egoistic premises and that central Kantian doctrines
can be rationally reconstructed on the basis of models that initially
seem anti-Kantian, see David Gauthier, "The Unity of Reason: A
Subversive Reinterpretation of Kant," *Ethics*, 96 (October 1985), pp.
74–88. (As Lisa Isaacson pointed out to me, the analysis presented in
this final section of the chapter will probably not help with the paradoxes of divine mercy, for it is probably not reasonable to view God's
morality as a result of a bargain He strikes with humanity in order to
advance His interests.)

21 "'You know, I have a confession to make,' said Sherman. He made
himself smile again. 'Until that sonofabitch came up here, I was thinking of blowing my brains out. Now I wouldn't dream of it. That would
solve all his problems, and he'd dine out on it for a month and be
damned sanctimonious while he was at it. He'd tell everybody how
we grew up together, and he'd shake that big round bubble head of
his. I think I'll invite those bastards' – he motioned toward [the mob

upbringing that both made me receptive to Kantianism in ethics and still makes me feel uneasy about the legitimacy of the hatreds to which I am by temperament given. If I did not experience such a tension within my own personality, I suspect that my perspective on these topics would be quite different – or perhaps that I would not even find these topics of any particular interest. When I encounter different perspectives in conversations with others or in literature that I read, I attempt to take them seriously and build them into my own theoretical account. I doubt, however, that I am totally successful in doing this, and I know that there are bound to be other perspectives (in our common life, in literature, and in other cultures) that I have yet to encounter and that may therefore fall very much outside the confines of my own way of conceptualizing the topics I have been investigating in my portions of this book.

I am sure that these are in part personal limitations, but I think that they are also limitations inherent in philosophy itself – at least on topics of this nature. Although most philosophers hate to admit it, Thomas Nagel is surely correct when he tells us that "philosophical ideas are acutely sensitive to individual temperament, and to wishes."[22] They are also deeply sensitive to one's own life experiences and to the imaginative literature one has read. One tries to overcome this subjectivity as much as one is able, for otherwise one's ideas would be nothing more than autobiography – likely to be of little interest to anyone except one's mother. And yet such subjectivity can never be totally overcome, nor would it be desirable if it could be; for, without some personal perspective, it would be unclear why one is bothering to think

in the] streets – 'on up here and let 'em dance the mazurka right over his big bubble head.'"

"'Ayyyyyy,' said Killian. 'That's better. Now you're turning fucking *Irish*. The Irish been living the last twelve hundred years on dreams of revenge. Now you're *talking*, bro'" (Tom Wolfe, *The Bonfire of the Vanities* [New York: Farrar, Straus, Giroux, 1987], p. 536).

22 Thomas Nagel, *The View from Nowhere* (New York: Oxford University Press, 1986), p. 10.

and write about certain topics at all and why one is commending them to others for their reflection. One must therefore simply hope that the personal perspective that informs one's philosophical reflections is sufficiently complex and profound that it will mesh with the complex and profound concerns of others and thus that it might provide them, not with the final truth on the matter at hand, but at least with a useful starting point for their own reflections – something to build on or to react against. Jean Hampton and I certainly have no higher hopes than this for the value of our reflections on forgiveness and mercy.

Index

Adams, Robert, 65n, 79n
Aeschylus, 106n
anger
  and forgiveness, 11
  and forms of hatred, 143–7
  and indignation, 56
  and insult, 44
  and resentment, 38, 54, 158
  see also retributive hatred
Anselm, Saint
  paradoxes of mercy, 168–9, 177,
    180–1
  see also equal protection paradox
apology, 24, 28
Aquinas, Saint Thomas, 8
Aristotle, 5n, 8, 18, 78, 109n, 146n
Augustine, Saint, 24
Axelrod, Robert, 95n

Bacon, Francis, 17n
Baier, Annette, 154n
bargaining model of moral
  conventions, 181–2
Beardsley, Elizabeth, 24n
Beck, Lewis White, 103n, 172n
Berger, Thomas, 106n
betrayal, 17
Bible, *see* New Testament, Old
  Testament
"bite-back" response, 54, 117–18,
  139
  see also punishment; retribution
Boswell, James, 35

Butler, Joseph, 16, 34, 37
  and definition of forgiveness, 15,
    20, 22, 35, 38, 43

Calvino, Italo, 184
Camelback rapist, 92, 120, 134,
  142
Camus, Albert, 1, 102, 103n
Card, Claudia, 170n, 171n
Cartesianism, 94n, 99
categorical imperative, *see*
  imperatives, categorical
change of heart, *see* forgiveness,
  change of heart in
Christianity, 4, 10, 11, 12, 18n, 22,
  30, 31, 86, 119–21, 153
  see also forgiveness, Christian
Coleman, Jules L., 107n, 177n
compassion, 173, 181
  and Christian tradition, 31
condemnation, 156–7
  and retribution, 117
condonation
  definition of, 40
  and forgiveness, 39, 40, 42, 83, 84,
    85, 148
Cosmus, Duke of Florence, 17
criminal law
  and forgiveness, 33
  and individuation, 170–2, 175
  and institutionalization of anger
    and hatred, 2–3, 33
  and justice, 152

187

Index

Index

Index

punishment
  and defeat of wrongdoer's cause,
    124–5
  as deterrent, 129, 139, 140
  and distributive justice, 114
  Hampton's definition of, 126
  as infliction of suffering, 126
  and institutionalized resentment, 8
  limits on, 127–8, 135–7
  and moral education, 113–14,
    129–30, 174
  as nullification of wrongdoer's
    claim to superiority
    (reassertion of victim's value),
    125–6, 128–31, 133–4
  and taking away advantage from
    wrong action, 114–16
  as vindicating value through
    protection, 138–43
  see also retribution; retributive
    hatred

ranking of persons, 45–9, 51, 53, 57,
    58, 70–3, 75–8, 81, 82, 145
  evidence for, 47–8, 50, 63–4, 66–70,
    137–8
  and resentment, 54–5, 57–60, 62–3,
    67, 71, 79–80, 148
  see also value of oneself; value of
    persons; worth, theories of
    human
Rawls, John, 93n, 101
recognition strategy
  malice as, 65–75, 105n, 119n, 137,
    145–6
  'neophyte', 65
  spite as, 65, 76–8
  'superstar', 64
  'unscrupulous', 62–3
repentance, 41
  as evidence of moral worth, 69, 83,
    154–5
  and forgiveness, 29–31, 41, 154n
resentment, 17, 29, 31, 78, 88, 104n

and anger, 54
cognitive understanding of, 5n, 38,
    54
and culpable wrongdoing, 18, 20,
    55
and defiance, 57–9
and demeaning treatment, 54–5
as different from indignation,
    56–60
and fear, 57, 150
forgiveness as forswearing of, 15,
    20–3, 33, 35, 36, 38–43, 64
Hampton's definition of, 59–60
and hatred, 60–1, 70–1, 94
and justification of retributive
    hatred, 148
overcoming of, 38, 39, 148
and personal defense, 15–16, 55,
    58
and self-respect, 16–17, 22, 93
as sign of weakness, 58, 93–4
and theories of human worth, 55,
    58
understood as different from
    "bite-back" response, 54
retribution
  and anger, 143–6, 205
  and "bite-back" response, 117–19
  as communication about
    wrongdoer's value, 123,
    125–8, 130, 138
  and diminishment of wrongdoer's
    self-value, 125, 126, 133–4
  and distributive justice, 114
  and egalitarian theories of human
    worth, 135, 137–8
  and forgiveness, 147, 157–8
  as foundational moral idea
    (deontological theory of),
    112–13, 123
  Hegel's theory of, 104, 114, 131,
    142
  Kant's theory of, 95n, 97–102, 107,
    131

192